Abbas Kiarostami: Interviews

Conversations with Filmmakers Series
Gerald Peary, General Editor

ABBAS KIAROSTAMI
INTERVIEWS

Edited by Monika Raesch

University Press of Mississippi / Jackson

The University Press of Mississippi is the scholarly publishing agency of the Mississippi Institutions of Higher Learning: Alcorn State University, Delta State University, Jackson State University, Mississippi State University, Mississippi University for Women, Mississippi Valley State University, University of Mississippi, and University of Southern Mississippi.

www.upress.state.ms.us

The University Press of Mississippi is a member of the Association of University Presses.

Copyright © 2023 by University Press of Mississippi
All rights reserved

First printing 2023
∞

Library of Congress Cataloging-in-Publication Data

Names: Raesch, Monika, editor.
Title: Abbas Kiarostami : interviews / Monika Raesch.
Other titles: Conversations with filmmakers series.
Description: Jackson : University Press of Mississippi, 2023. | Series: Conversations with filmmakers series | Includes bibliographical references and index.
Identifiers: LCCN 2022048770 (print) | LCCN 2022048771 (ebook) |
  ISBN 9781496844866 (hardback) | ISBN 9781496844873 (trade paperback) |
  ISBN 9781496844880 (epub) | ISBN 9781496844897 (epub) |
  ISBN 9781496844903 (pdf) | ISBN 9781496844910 (pdf)
Subjects: LCSH: Kiarostami, Abbas—Interviews. | Kiarostami, Abbas—Criticism and interpretation. | Motion picture producers and directors—Iran—Interviews. | Motion pictures—Production and direction.
Classification: LCC PN1998.3.K58 A222 2023 (print) | LCC PN1998.3.K58 (ebook) |
  DDC 791.4302/33092—dc23/eng/20230120
LC record available at https://lccn.loc.gov/2022048770
LC ebook record available at https://lccn.loc.gov/2022048771

British Library Cataloging-in-Publication Data available

Contents

Introduction   vii

Chronology   xliii

Filmography   xlvii

The Camera of Art—An Interview with Abbas Kiarostami   3
  Miriam Rosen / 1991

Abbas Kiarostami by Akram Zaatari   10
  BOMB / 1995

Abbas Kiarostami Interview   16
  UNESCO Courier / 1995

A Fax Conversation between Jonathan Rosenbaum and Abbas Kiarostami   20
  Jonathan Rosenbaum / 1997

Between Dreams and Reality   24
  UNESCO Courier / 1998

Interview with Abbas Kiarostami for a Book by Jonathan Rosenbaum   29
  Jonathan Rosenbaum and Mehrnaz Saeed-Vafa / 1998

Nature Has No Culture: The Photographs of Abbas Kiarostami   34
  Shiva Balaghi and Anthony Shadid / 2000

Meeting Abbas Kiarostami—The 24th Montreal World Film Festival   38
  Peter Rist / 2000

Abbas Kiarostami—The Poetry of Everyday Life   42
  Mazzino Montinari / 2002

Interview: Abbas Kiarostami   44
   Ulrich Köhler and Benjamin Heisenberg / 2003

Abbas Kiarostami at Bard College with *Five*, March 4, 2007   50
   Scott MacDonald / 2007

Shirin as Described by Kiarostami   61
   Khatereh Khodaei / 2009

Certifying the Copy: An Interview with Abbas Kiarostami   65
   Aaron Cutler / 2010

Kiarostami's View into Iran's Future   72
   ORF.at / 2011

A Very, Very, Very Bad Situation   75
   Ulrike Timm and Waltraud Tschirner / 2011

Communication Is the Most Selfless of All Art Forms   79
   Andreas Busche / 2011

"The Ideal Me and the Real Me"   82
   Arash T. Riahi / 2016

Coda   88

Additional Resources   93

Index   99

Introduction

This volume provides a range of interviews with Kiarostami—starting in 1991—to provide readers with the opportunity to explore the evolution of the filmmaker across the decades. Due to Kiarostami's untimely passing, the last two interviews in this volume are not interviews. "The Ideal Me and the Real Me," written by Arash T. Riahi, is a eulogy, published in November 2016 in *ray Filmmagazin*, an Austrian publication. This piece was selected as it shares some of the late filmmaker's actions and approaches to life that have not been covered in the interviews, illuminating the person—as opposed to only the filmmaker—Kiarostami. The coda of this book provides an excerpt from filmmaking workshops Kiarostami gave over the course of his career. Reprinted from *Lessons with Kiarostami*, edited by Paul Cronin, the last word in this volume is given to Kiarostami, to permit us—the readers—to listen to him as directly as possible, as he shares arguably timeless advice for any filmmaker.

Most prominently, the selection of interviews is impacted by the COVID-19 pandemic. As the world experienced variations of lockdowns and many people faced unemployment, the ability to receive permissions to reprint interviews in this volume was also significantly impacted. Looking at the set of interviews presented here brings fond memories, reminding me of the kind email conversations I had with authors and rights holders of the interviews. They kept me hopeful and reminded me that even though we didn't see many other people in person at that time, we were all still here, still passionate about film and wanting to share our appreciation for the art form. Unfortunately, due to some journals being forced to close their doors for an extended time period, some interviews were simply unavailable during the production phase of this book. Lastly, interviews have also been reprinted in other books; these were intentionally excluded here to avoid duplication with other publications. (Please see the books section in this volume's additional resources for a list of resources.)[1]

Throughout the introduction, I draw on a variety of sources, such as excerpts from behind-the-scenes documentaries, to provide additional quotations by the late filmmaker that offer information on a different aspect of filmmaking not included in the interviews. Most apparent, the interviews reprinted in this book were conducted after the release of a piece of work. This means that their focus is primarily on the respective finished piece and not on the production process. The documentary resources provide insight into the actual process of making decisions on a set—such as on directing cast and on the art of framing a shot—all of which have a direct impact on the finished product.

While the interviews provide a glimpse into Kiarostami's works and thought processes over the decades, regarding the films, availability of Kiarostami's works is varied. Some of his short films are distributed as special features on DVDs of his feature films. YouTube also features some of his works. The limitation of the latter is that at times one cannot know whether it is a genuine copy. In the 1990s and 2000s, films that were available in the United States were distributed by an Iranian distributor based in California. The subtitles were limited—some did not have any—and reliability of translation was uncertain. On the other hand, many of his films were available, including early shorts. Nowadays, many of his works are distributed by the Criterion Collection. Concerns with subtitles have disappeared. Overall, the availability and quality of the films naturally impacted the interaction with the works, by critics and scholars as well as general audiences from their respective original distribution until today. You may notice that a film is referred to by different titles across interviews, such as *Taste of Cherry* also being called *A Taste of Cherry* and *The Taste of Cherry*. Similarly, some character names are spelled with minor variations. Direct quotes from films may also differ from the version you may be familiar with, signaling that a different copy of a respective film was used. In this book, the citations of films provide current distributor information of Kiarostami films. However, these are not always the versions that were used in the interviews or this introduction.

Approaching Filmmaking

> Artists yearn to communicate. That's what makes them artists. They become sick if they are unable to share their dreams. (*Lessons* 89)

Kiarostami asked audiences to discover *everything* in a film—that is, to be present and to engage with the visuals and audio he selected and arranged. Further, to experience his films without the goal of packaging them in summary statements, but to develop an understanding of life—whether in general, in a particular part of the world, or in a given situation. Jonathan Rosenbaum noted in an interview that Kiarostami was not a cinephile himself; he took inspiration from the world rather than from other films (*Abbas Kiarostami: The Art of Living* 02:33–02:41). Italian Cesare Zavattini said in *Some Ideas on the Cinema* (originally published in 1953, edited from an interview recorded in 1952), "While we are interested in the reality around us and want to know it directly, reality in American films is unnaturally filtered, 'purified,' and comes out at one or two removes. In America, lack of subjects for films causes a crisis, but with us such a crisis is impossible. One cannot be short of themes while there is still plenty of reality. Any hour of the day, any place, any person, is a subject for narrative if the narrator is capable of observing and illuminating all these collective elements by exploring their interior value" (218).

Kiarostami acknowledged his fondness for Italian neorealism (Aufderheide 32). During a conversation with Richard Peña, part of an Indiana University Cinema (IU Cinema) event, he said: "Neorealism did a great service to cinema. It showed us that there is another type of cinema. We can make films about the people around us and hold up the mirror to ourselves" (Palmer 4). In the article "Certifying the Copy: An Interview with Abbas Kiarostami" (originally published in *Cineaste* and provided in this volume), coauthor Aaron Cutler categorizes Kiarostami's film *Certified Copy* as "a genre synthesis" that includes "mid-movement neorealism." While Kiarostami creates a reality in his films, it is an ambiguous one. "[Kiarostami] likes to distill reality into something at its barest form. . . . You can really capture a moment and start meditating and start contemplating on that moment," says fellow filmmaker and academic Jamsheed Akrami (*Abbas Kiarostami: The Art of Living* 37:14–37:33). (While Akrami said this in relation to Kiarostami's photography, I feel that it can also be applied to his video work.)

Can we accept a moment as is, embrace the ambiguity, and see its beauty in the way Kiarostami presented it? That is a challenge Kiarostami arguably provided us with in every one of his films (and his other artistic works, such as poetry and photography). In a weeklong workshop, he provided the following example as to his preference for leaving gaps for the audience:

> If a story is missing its final page, we are forced to guess what happened to our hero, what decisions he made. It's as if the author is letting his readers complete the story themselves. At the end of my film *The Report*, a couple with marital problems is in a hospital room. She has attempted suicide and is in bed. He is on a chair next to her, where he sits throughout the night. The next morning he sees that his wife's eyes are open, that she is alive. He picks up his jacket and leaves. The last shot of the film is of the hospital's front doors as this man walks out, gets into his car, and drives away. An ending like that gives me the opportunity to avoid answering questions and, instead, pose them. The audience is forced to make up its own mind about what happens to these two people. A film with an open ending is more believable than one with a definite solid and sealed-off resolution. What film starts at the beginning of a character's life and ends with the end of that life? Everyone has a past and future we never see. This workshop will finish and we will all go home, but the ideas we have been talking

about will continue to work us over. There is no definitive closure to our experiences here this week. A story starts before we encounter it and concludes long after we have turned away. (*Lessons* 19)

Respecting this filmmaker's desire to give agency to the audience, this introduction to the Kiarostami volume in the Conversations with Filmmakers Series is not meant to provide a definitive summary of Kiarostami's body of work and his works' impact on the industry. The goal of this introduction is to provide information of Kiarostami's life and his films, but leave it up to the reader to make (individualized) meaning and/or create summaries relating to the filmmaker and his body of work, such as which themes are most important in his work. This approach would narrow meaning instantly, which goes against Kiarostami's wish for the audience to create meaning. Therefore, this introduction is divided into subsections that cover his work(s) from different perspectives but tries to avoid limiting meaning. It does not need to be read in order, beginning to end. You—the reader—are invited to read the pieces in any order you wish and to draw your own conclusions. (Yes, this is an indirect reference to Kiarostami's "An Unfinished Cinema"; it is the focus of the next subsection of this introduction.) I hope that this aids the reader in personalizing their experience of the text.

The Unfinished Cinema

For the Centenary of Cinema, celebrated in Paris in 1995, Kiarostami wrote the now-famous text "An Unfinished Cinema," which encapsulated his ideas for the role of the cinema audience. Part of the essay follows:

> Originally, I thought that the lights went out in a movie theatre so that we could see the images on the screen better. Then I looked a little closer at the audience settling comfortably into the seats and saw that there was a much more important reason: the darkness allowed the members of the audience to isolate themselves from others and be alone. They were both with others and distant from them.
>
> When we reveal a film's world to members of an audience, they each learn to create their own world through the wealth of their own experience.
>
> [. . .]
>
> I believe in a type of cinema that gives greater possibilities and time to its audience. A half-created cinema, an unfinished cinema that attains completion through the creative spirit of the audience, so resulting in hundreds of films. It belongs to the members of that audience and corresponds to their world.
>
> The world of each work, of each film recounts a new truth. In the darkened theatre, we give everyone the chance to dream and to express his dream freely.

[. . .]
In cinema's next century, respect of the audience as an intelligent and constructive element is inevitable. To attain this, one must perhaps move away from the concept of the audience as the absolute master. The director must also be the audience of his own film.

For one hundred years, cinema has belonged to the filmmaker. Let us hope that now the time has come for us to implicate the audience in its second century.[2]

Kiarostami called for giving power to the audience, for making them an active collaborator in a film's meaning-making process. The spotlight should not be held by a director alone for their artistic genius but should be shared with the audience, who bring a film to life by interacting with the product the filmmaker provided. The positioning of the audience as a collaborator adds power to the consumer. Kiarostami films do not offer one correct interpretation of the narrative. A gap can be filled in different ways. Depending on how one fills it, the next gap may be filled in a way that fits with the first one. Each audience member must make the story their own, by filling in holes with something that makes sense, using their own life experience, world view, and knowledge. In the end, they have created a film *together with* Kiarostami. Arguably, this is the key reason why it is difficult to summarize a Kiarostami film to someone else, as we must divorce the product—the actual film—from our own individual interpretations of what we saw and what it all means. Kiarostami describes it as "giv[ing] everyone the chance to dream and to express [their] dream freely." For Kiarostami, using music sparingly relates to this wish to give the audience agency. He says:

> Music is a perfect art by itself. It's very powerful and impressive. I dare not try to compete with music in my films. I can't engage in that kind of activity as the use of music has a great deal of emotional charge and burden, and I do not want to place this on my spectator. Music plays on the spectators' emotions, makes them excited or sad, and takes them through a veritable emotional roller coaster like ups and downs and I respect my spectator too much to do that. (Mahdi par. 56)

His wish for a text that is more open to interpretation can create challenges though. A tension may surface between the filmmaker who wants to keep meaning ambiguous to some extent and the film critics, scholars, and consumers who want to summarize and critique a person's work. For example, in the forum, "In Dialogue with Kiarostami," the ending of his film *Taste of Cherry* (1997) is discussed (Mahdi pars. 29–34). Throughout the film, the protagonist, Mr. Badii, had contemplated suicide. In the final minutes of the film, he enters his self-dug grave. A thunderstorm develops and passes overhead. Next, a cut to daytime, and the actor who portrays Mr. Badii is seen walking around, smoking a cigarette. The audience is wondering whether he survived or whether this is the actor in between takes. Kiarostami created confusion with the film's ending and does not clarify the situation; instead, the closing credits begin. Why did Kiarostami take this approach? He explains:

> I didn't want spectators emotionally involved in this film. In this film, I tell you very little about Mr. Badii, I tell you very little about what his life is about, why he wanted to commit suicide, what his story is. I didn't want the spectators [to] get engaged in those aspects of his life. For that purpose I had to keep Mr. Badii away from the audience. So he is a distant actor in a way. First I thought to end the movie at the point when he laid down on his grave but later I changed my mind. I was uncomfortable to end it at that point because I was very concerned, and am always concerned, about my spectators. I do not want to take them hostage. I do not want to take their emotions hostage. It is very easy for a filmmaker to control the emotions of spectators but I do not like that. I do not want to see my audience as innocent children whose emotions are easily manipulable.
>
> I was afraid that if I ended the movie where Mr. Badii laid down on his grave the spectator would be left with a great deal of sadness. Even though I didn't think the scene was really that sad, I was afraid that it would come out as such. For that reason I decided to have the next episode where we have the camera running as Mr. Badii was walking around. I wanted to remind spectators that this was really a film and that they shouldn't think about this as a reality. They should not become involved emotionally. This is much like some of our grandmothers who told us stories, some with happy and some with sad endings. But they always at the end would have a Persian saying which went like this "but after all it is just a story!" (pars. 33–34)[3]

When I was a student, I asked my film professor about this ending, communicating similar confusion. I wanted to know what had happened to Mr. Badii, used to receiving narrative closure thanks to my diet of Hollywood films growing up. My professor explained Kiarostami's intention and put it in the following visual: he asked why I (likely) cared about Mr. Badii more than about my neighbors.

At the forum, Kiarostami continued explaining:

> The very last episode reminds me of the continuation of life, that life goes on, and here the audience is confronted with the reality they had hoped that Mr. Badii would be alive and there he is a part of nature and nature still continues and life goes on even without Mr. Badii. And if one could really think about being or not being present in life, or if one thinks about it in terms of the real implication of such presence, one might not in fact engage in committing suicide at all. The person committing

suicide might think that s/he is taking revenge from the society, nature, life, powers to be, and so on. But s/he don't realize that after a suicide life still goes on and things stay the way they are. I could interpret this in a different way. If my audience is as creative as I imagine them to be, they can take this in a variety of interpretations and I can sit here and every time make a different interpretation of it, as every time one can creatively reinterpret the reality. (par. 36)

Kiarostami connects the choice for the ending with his aim for an unfinished cinema that permits interpretation and reinterpretation. He elaborates, speaking about the process of moviemaking overall:

I have to say that what we produce is subject to interpretation, taste, and preferences. Movies, like other cultural objects, are interpretive objects. There is a meaning in them intended by the author, a meaning understood by the audience, a meaning generated as a result of the interaction of these different meanings. For instance, a critic did not like *Taste of Cherry* because he didn't see the grave and he wanted me to actually focus on the concrete grave. But he missed the point that I had so many scenes in which I depicted the grave in a symbolic way. [Kiarostami now refers to a different scene in the film where Mr. Badii watches happenings at a work site.] Every time the soil was being poured down by the truck, Mr. Badii was seeing his own grave. In every downpouring of the soil and gravel, he was imagining himself under their weight. (par. 50)

The fact that any media is based on the interpretation magnifies the importance of a consumer's meaning-making process. Whether an audience member enjoys a film likely depends on whether they felt that a filmmaker communicated similarly to their own communication style. If something is similar to our own, we get the sense that we understand the creator of the message more easily and fully. If we consume media that we have difficulty making sense of, we will likely find it less appealing.

David Sterritt posited that Kiarostami "never drew sharp lines between cinema that tells and cinema that reveals and simply shows" (94). (Sterritt made the distinction between "telling," "revealing," and "showing" in the memoriam piece "The Element of Chance," published in *Film Comment* in fall 2016.) Kiarostami's way of sharing information often had little in common with Hollywood narrative, with storytelling that incorporates a clear and easy-to-follow storyline that limits ambiguity.

As you read the interviews in this volume, you will come across several instances where Kiarostami says something similar to not wanting to answer a question directly, but if needed he can do so. For instance, in the piece "Certifying the Copy: An Interview with Abbas Kiarostami," coauthor Aaron Cutler desires a direct answer as to how much an answer to a question was about Kiarostami himself and not (only) a discussion of a movie character. Kiarostami responds: "I have answered this indirectly, but if you'd like me to answer it directly, I can." In the interview "A Very, Very, Very Bad Situation" for *Deutschlandfunk*, the interviewer praises Kiarostami as part of a longer question. He does not want to confirm her statement, as he considers this awkward, and continues with, "Let me say something that may be an indirect answer to your question." These are examples of the negotiation of meaning of respective pieces of work and their reception between the parties. Kiarostami desires to leave some of his work and his answers open to interpretation, while interviewers desire precise answers that provide definitive meaning.

While Kiarostami desired gaps in the narrative, he also saw his possibility of creating specific meaning to "intervene in a problem of social class" (Rice 167). For instance, *Through the Olive Trees* (1994) explores the question of whether marriage between people of different economic statuses would benefit the people and society as a whole. Kiarostami explained, "Filmmaking gives me the opportunity to forget about reality sometimes, to break away from it and dream from time to time. And in my opinion the audience has the same feelings at that moment because they share the same desire to change reality." Society evolves continuously. Film can be used to dream about and explore how a change in ideology may impact lives, with the goal to evolve life for the better. "I don't think it's the role of art to judge. The role of art is to make people think" (*Abbas Kiarostami: Truth and Dreams* 45:07–45:12). Michael Ciment, from *Positif*, summarizes that Kiarostami's cinema is "both a sensual cinema . . . and at the same time a cinema of thought" (*Abbas Kiarostami: The Art of Living* 04:41–4:50).

For Kiarostami, creating films was a way to communicate ideas. In the 1995 interview for the *UNESCO Courier*—which is reprinted in this volume—he exclaims, "Making films is something that I have to do. It's like dreaming; it comes naturally, it fulfills a need." He elaborates in the documentary *Roads of Kiarostami*:

> The road is the expression of a man's journey, in search of provisions. The road is the illustration of the soul that has no peace, and the body is the pack animal of the soul that carries it from place to place. Whoever neglects his pack animal will never reach his journey's end, but the journey of man continues. Our roads are like ourselves, sometimes stony, sometimes paved, sometimes winding, sometimes straight, and the path we draw on earth are like scratches upon it. And we have other ways inside us, ways of sadness, ways of joy, ways of love, ways of thought, ways of escape, and sometimes ways which spring from hatred, ways which destroy us, ways which go nowhere, ways without a conclusion like a stagnant river. The road is a man's confession

of the places he is fleeing from, the places he is heading. The road is life, the road is man and man's road, however small, flows on the page of existence, sometimes without conclusion, sometimes victorious.[4]

Throughout this book, Kiarostami provides insight into his (artistic) frame of mind. In the conversation at Bard College ("Abbas Kiarostami at Bard College with *Five*, March 4, 2007"), Kiarostami uses an analogy of his work being created on and set on small roads as opposed to the highway. The small roads represent independent work; the highway stands for the mainstream film industry. He says that even when making his films, the highway is not forgotten. "The highway gives us the opportunity to know where we are: we look at the highway so that we don't get lost." In the interview "Abbas Kiarostami—The Poetry of Everyday Life," Kiarostami describes his work from an artist's perspective, explaining how funding of his films does not impact his artistic vision.

A Brief Overview of Kiarostami's Career as a Filmmaker

As the filmography shows, Kiarostami's early works were created for Kanun Parvaresh Fekri, the Institute for the Intellectual Development of Children and Young Adults, for which Kiarostami worked. The reason the institute is also known as "Kanoon" (or Kanun) is that its location was in the city of Kanoon (or Kanun) (Knox par. 4). In the article "Cacti Blossom in the Desert: Some Short Films of Abbas Kiarostami," Jim Knox provides summaries of Kiarostami's early films, such as *Two Solutions for One Problem* (1975), which includes havoc between children that features, among others, "wreckage of broken rulers and pens, ripped clothing, [a] black eye" (par. 8). Working at Kanun meant that a focus on children was ever-present throughout the films. The 1998 interview "Between Reality and Dreams"—reprinted in this book—opens with Kiarostami speaking about his beginnings working with the film medium.

From the second film onward, Kiarostami not only worked as director but is also credited for the screenplays and sometimes as coeditor or editor and producer. Having different roles in the production of a film at the beginning of his filmmaking career permitted him to experience various areas that are all shaping the final product early on. The films he made were a mixture of shorts—for instance, *So Can I* (1975), with a running time of four minutes—and feature works, such as *The Report* (1977), which is 112 minutes long. Kiarostami received his first award, the Jury Special Award, for *Bread and Alley* (1970), at the 5th Tehran International Festival of Films for Children and Young Adults in 1970. (The chronology section in this book provides a more detailed overview of Kiarostami's life, including the years he worked at Kanun.)

Working at Kanun at the start of his career appears to have been a perfect fit for Kiarostami. Regarding children and childhood, Kiarostami has said:

> The indirect aim of creating art is to retreat deep into childhood games. That's where real joy lies. As soon as a child discovers something he wants to achieve beyond the sheer pleasure of the game itself, the moment he becomes competitive, the game is over. At its best, artistic work is a childlike process where elements of the unconscious grow in strength, eventually overwhelming the conscious. Re-connecting with youthful impulses isn't a choice for an artist. It's a necessity.
>
> I'm glad there are no grown-ups in my life telling me what to do. These days, when I spend time with my family and they start talking about one thing or another, often I take my leave and join the children in the other room. I find most adult conversations uninteresting. The most wonderful period in the life of a human being is childhood, when encountering even the most miniscule things becomes a process of radical exploration. It's a pity we leave those times behind so quickly. (*Lessons* 89)

His works bring to light children's dreams and sense of adventure. In *The Traveler* (1974), a boy, Qassem, finds ways to save up money to buy a bus ticket to see his favorite soccer team play.[5] In *And Life Goes On* (1991), the adult protagonist is paired with his son, adding a child's perspective throughout their journey. In the film, an unnamed filmmaker drives to the towns of Koker and Poshteh to find out whether the two main boys of the film *Where's the Friend's House?* (1987) survived a real-life earthquake. Arguably, the two characters represent Kiarostami and one of his sons. They are showcasing the dynamics of an adult who is focused on achieving a goal and his child who naturally explores along the way.

Kiarostami has said that he tried "to look at the world and life from a child's point of view" (*Interview from 1997*).[6] Early on in *And Life Goes On*, when the boy needs to step out of the car for a bio break, he gets distracted by a grasshopper. He catches the grasshopper and brings it into the car, as a third passenger. The father is not pleased. He asks his son to throw it out the window. The son refuses at first, wanting to raise the grasshopper as his pet. Eventually, he ejects the animal via the window. The adult could not position himself into the child's perspective. He is on a specific quest, and that makes all other things unimportant. Throughout the film, when the father speaks to locals, always with the intention of finding out about the boys, his son explores the rubble. The boy takes in his environments for what they are, not framing them through one question only (whether the boys survived). Eventually, his dad does have moments where he puts the quest aside (however temporarily) and takes in his surroundings for what they are. One such moment is when the father sees a wall painting, situated on a wall of a collapsed house. The painting survived the earthquake, though one big crack runs through it. Kiarostami shows the protagonist finding a moment of physical non-movement. Nature is framed through an open gap where a door once stood. The painting is situated on the wall space to the left of the door opening. What the father thinks as he looks at the painting and the doorframe is left to the audience to imagine. Eventually, the father does go to the remains of the house and steps through the door space by stepping over the collapsed door. He takes time to look around from left to right. He steps back over the door and approaches the painting. Again, he stands still and gazes at the work of art. What may be implied via the slowly changing behavior of the father is that he does learn from his son on this journey, regardless of whether he is conscious of it. Stopping to change perspectives does not mean one is straying from one's goal. The goal was the original reason for the journey and is still to be reached, but not seeing anything else along the journey means missing out on life.

Children don't miss out; they notice "the most miniscule things" and explore them (*Lessons* 89). That's how we learn, and this learning is just as important as formal learning in a school setting that children engage in once they reach school age. This may be the message Kiarostami intended to send, but it may also not have been. He leaves a gap for the audience to engage. Fellow filmmaker Professor Jamsheed Akrami suggests in an interview that having to make films with children meant that Kiarostami "discovered them" in a completely new way (*Interview from 1997*).[7] Kiarostami elaborates that children are "nicer" and "easygoing" and that "their viewpoints are often more accurate [than those of adults] and more interesting."

Seventeen years after making his first film, the Farabi Film Foundation became a coproducer together with Kanun Parvaresh Fekri on *Where's the Friend's House?* (1987). This film would lead to worldwide recognition. By the late 1980s, Kiarostami began to collect international awards. In 1989, he was awarded the Bronze Leopard and the Barclay Jury Prize at the 42nd Locarno International Film Festival in Switzerland for *Where's the Friend's House?* He also received the Best Film Award for this movie at the International Film Festival of the Royal Film Archive of Belgium in 1990. His first Best Directing award followed in 1991 at the 5th Dunkerque International Film Festival in France for *Close-Up* (1990). This film is viewed as one of the key films of the Iranian New Wave. Numerous awards followed over the years and decades. Among them, Director of the Year by the *Variety International Film Guide* in 1996 and the coveted Palme d'Or for Best Film at the 50th Cannes International Film Festival in 1997 for *Taste of Cherry* (1997). This film would be awarded best (foreign) film of the year 1997 in numerous countries, including in the US by the National Society of Film Critics and *Time Magazine*. Also in 1997, UNESCO awarded him the Federico Fellini Gold Medal for his film career.

The welcoming reception of Kiarostami in the Western world, especially in France early on in his career, created a path to his career. With funding for many films coming from the French production company mk2 Productions (now known as mk2 Films), he was provided with freedom as to the creative process and content of his works in contrast to Iranian officials approving his scripts. Other Western production companies would also fund films. (Please see the filmography for details.)

In the 1990s, Kiarostami also began creating segments of films that were codirected. For *A Propos de Nice, La Suite* (1995), he directed the segment "Repérages." Eventually, he would codirect the feature film *Tickets* (2005) with Ken Loach and Ermanno Olmi. Three successful and acclaimed directors come together to share a film, to give one another space to express their own creativity while still having to ensure that the film plays as a harmonious whole.

Toward the end of his career, Kiarostami could not make films in Iran anymore; he shot in France and Japan, respectively. The transition to shooting in a foreign land was not easy. In 2001, Akrami asked Kiarostami about making films outside of Iran, wondering about the confidence level of leaving one's familiar space. By that time, Kiarostami had shot the documentary *ABC Africa* (2001) in Uganda. Kiarostami replied that:

> Making films is always wrought with a lot of concerns. The thought of changing our turf could double your concerns. You keep thinking whether it's the right thing to do. Logically, it would make perfect sense, since the language of film, or arts in general, is essentially a universal language. Our audiences relate to our films through subtitles.... But I just don't feel comfortable with the idea. I am supposed to make a film in Japan. But anytime I think about it, I feel overcome by a sense of anxiety. (*A Walk with Kiarostami* 22:54–23:40)

He added that he didn't know the reason for this feeling. His status as a celebrated filmmaker was not a factor. He continued, "But I just don't know whether it would be right for me to work somewhere else or not. Logically, it makes sense. Intuitively, it doesn't" (24:19–24:23).

Several interviews in this volume illuminate this aspect of his career, including "Certifying the Copy: An Interview with Abbas Kiarostami" and "Communication Is the Most Selfless of All Art Forms." The 2011 interview "A Very, Very, Very Bad Situation" also illuminates the volatile relationship the Iranian government and Kiarostami had throughout his career. The article suggests that the Iranian theocracy could use filmmakers to their advantage when it suited them; at other times, it could oppose their work and enforce consequences. The interview "Kiarostami's View into Iran's Future" discusses the situation of

Kiarostami's colleague Dschafar Panahi, who was arrested and threatened with a prison sentence.

While Kiarostami was not jailed or ordered under house arrest during his career as some of his colleagues were, he also had an uneasy relationship with the government. When Kiarostami won the Golden Palm at the Cannes Film Festival in 1997, in the eyes of some, he behaved inappropriately at the awards ceremony. On stage, he kissed actress Catherine Deneuve on the cheek. Stuart Jeffries elaborates in "Landscapes of the Mind": "The fact that a man had kissed a woman to whom he was not married in public offended conservative Iranian sensibilities so much that the release of the film was thwarted. Kiarostami stayed away from his homeland until the storm subsided" (par. 3). Jamsheed Akrami summarized the happenings as "the most shining moment in Iranian cinema [being] lost in the scandal of the kiss" (Jeffries par. 3).

While the incident at Cannes did not focus on his work, Kiarostami has said that the government officials "don't understand my films and so prevent them being shown just in case there is a message they don't want to get out. They tend to support films that are stylistically very different from mine—melodramas" (Jeffries par. 4). Later in the article, Kiarostami adds: "The government doesn't just own the cinemas, but also the means of production, so I have to work around them. Even if that means editing at night" (par. 9). While the summary of his career up to this point may suggest that he had not experienced problems with governmental oversight in his early career, this was not the case.

In 1977, Kiarostami was commissioned to make a short for the education ministry. A cut of his work was pre-screened, and cuts were demanded "to suppress images of women wearing a hijab, since these women were opposed to the Shah's modernization" (par. 13). Kiarostami refused to make the cuts himself but offered the ministry to perform them themselves. As a result, "the film was never screened." Two years later, his film *Case #1, Case #2* (1979) was also censored from screening due to the Iranian Revolution, which resulted in the Islamic Republic (par. 14). While Kiarostami tried to alter the film so it would receive distribution—he reshot scenes and reedited the film—"the government banned it because its presumed message was deemed subversive and because some of the commentaries came from members of political parties (communist, democratic national front) which had been declared illegal" (par. 15). While the original halt to the film's distribution—the Iranian Revolution—could be summarized as the film having been completed at the wrong moment in time, the eventual censorship of the work even after significant changes had been made illustrates the power of the government to control messages it would permit in films.[8]

In another interview that accompanied the release of the 1997 film *Taste of Cherry*, Kiarostami explained that after the Iranian revolution, censorship "should mostly be considered religious restrictions" (*Interview from 1997*).⁹ He "adjusts to the circumstances" along with his colleagues. "In my mind, censorship isn't something that bothers us terribly, because we found our ways to counter it." In the past decade, conditions for filmmakers in Iran had deteriorated significantly though. As previously mentioned, eventually he could no longer shoot feature films in his own country. *Certified Copy* (2010) and *Like Someone in Love* (2012) were shot on other continents. Even if his intuition told him not to shoot work elsewhere, eventually he no longer had a choice. While this made his work significantly more difficult, Kiarostami appeared to have a positive outlook: "Art is born of difficult or unfavorable circumstances for the artist." Simultaneously, he also felt that there was no purpose in discussing censorship: "There's no advantage in it"—yet in many interviews with Western journalists and in Q&A sessions with audiences it was an inevitable topic that he had to confront. To hear Kiarostami's perspective on working under restrictions at the time directly from him and uncut, the next paragraph features a longer answer.

In 1998, Kiarostami was a guest at a public forum of the Wexner Center for the Arts at Ohio State University in Columbus, Ohio. Preceding the screening of *Taste of Cherry* (1997), he engaged in a conversation during which censorship was one topic. An audience member felt that "a lot of great art is coming out of oppressive cultures or regimes" (Mahdi par. 29). The audience member wondered how much Kiarostami would be the same and how much his work would be the same were he to live and make movies in the West. (To avoid potential confusion for readers, this forum took place prior to Kiarostami making films outside of Iran.) Kiarostami responded:

> I like to use the phrase restrictive to describe the conditions I work under rather than oppressive and I understand that oppressive means many different things under different contexts but for us as artists and filmmakers what we are dealing with are the realities of restrictions and I like to approach it from that angle. I look at these restrictions not in the context of the film alone but in the broader context of life. For me these restrictions exist everywhere and have always been there. Life in the East has never been without them. We have to always live within certain boundaries. Life is the combination and movement between restriction and freedom—the field of action is limited, the field of power is limited, when we were kids we were always told what we could do and what we couldn't and how far we could go in doing things we could.
>
> The best example I can give for this concept is when our teachers told us to do a composition for the class. When he gave us a topic, we would write about that topic and come up with something worthwhile. But when he did not specify the topic and left us free to choose our own, we usually couldn't come up with something worth writing about. We needed to be told what the boundaries and restrictions were. This has been

the nature of our society and has been replicated in the realities of our film industry. For instance, during the first four years of the Iranian revolution, there was a great deal of chaos in the film industry because not many rules were set yet. Interestingly enough, most of the Iranian movie-makers didn't produce much during this time though a great deal could have been done. No one used the opportunity because everyone was waiting to find out what the restrictions were!

Most of the time we seek an excuse for running away from the responsibility. Restrictions give us this kind of excuse. Therefore, unfortunately, we seek energy from these boundaries set for us. I don't want to imply that these limitations are good and should be there, but we have been brought up with these and it is in our mentality. This is not limited to my profession—it's in every profession; creativity is a necessity and limitation makes people more creative. I have a friend who is an architect. He tells me that he is at his best professionally when he designs structures for odd lots because these lands do not fit into the normal pattern and he has to work within a great deal of limitations. So, he must be creative and he enjoys this. It is these restrictions that provide an opportunity for people to be creative. (pars. 30–32)

Even though Kiarostami had to tell stories in different countries and cultures, they are his. Possibly, the difficult circumstances under which he produced his art also shaped the evolution of his work over the decades. Some aspects of our lives are out of our control. Kiarostami has said:

When you take a tree that is rooted in the ground, and transfer it from one place to another, the tree will no longer bear fruit. And if it does, the fruit will not be as good as it was in its original place. This is a rule of nature. I think if I had left my country, I would be the same as the tree. (Rice 202)

Arguably, the films Kiarostami shot outside of his home country are a variation on the original flavor and taste just as good. They illuminate another side of Kiarostami, the filmmaker, one that would not have come to light if the circumstances had been different. He could not change things outside of his control; his filmmaking had to develop in unforeseen ways. In addition to the interviews listed previously in this section, the topics politics and governmental oversight are part of the conversation in the following interviews: "Between Dreams and Reality," "Meeting Abbas Kiarostami—The 24th Montreal World Film Festival," "Abbas Kiarostami—The Poetry of Everyday Life," and "Abbas Kiarostami at Bard College with *Five*, March 4, 2007."

Regardless of circumstances, Kiarostami's status in the film world was one of continued celebration. He received honors that are presented to someone with an established, successful career. Besides receiving awards at film festivals,

Kiarostami became a British Film Institute fellow in 2005. The BFI Fellowship "is awarded to individuals in recognition of their outstanding contribution to film or television culture" ("BFI Fellows" par. 1). Kiarostami was also appointed president of the jury for the Caméra d'Or Award at the Cannes Film Festival in 2005. He had come full circle, from winning an award in the previous decade for *Taste of Cherry* (1997) to presiding over what is arguably the most important film jury in the world.

Godfrey Cheshire provides his perspective on the second half of Kiarostami's career in his 2017 essay for *Film Comment*, "In the City of Abbas." Cheshire writes:

> Remarkably, after that decade [referring to the 1990s] Kiarostami seemed uninterested in maintaining his status as the elevated auteur of celluloid Iranian masterpieces. He embraced low-budget digital feature-filmmaking (*Ten* and the documentary *ABC Africa*), made experimental films (*Five*, *Shirin*, and his final feature, *24 Frames*), and dramatic features in foreign countries and languages (*Certified Copy* in Italy, *Like Someone in Love* in Japan; at his death he was preparing a feature to be made in China). (55)

Cheshire implied realities of the film industry and of Kiarostami. Keeping a status that is aspired to but difficult to achieve—that is, being an auteur—means adhering to expectations of those that awarded the status. By making films significantly different from the ones that resulted in the auteur label, Kiarostami permitted critics and scholars to reconsider him and the value of his works. By shooting films in different techniques and in various countries, Kiarostami opened the door to critics and scholars to cast their praises elsewhere.[10]

The Question of Reality in Cinema

> Whenever we see real people who have appeared in films, they seem much smaller than their screen size or the reality they represented on the screen. Or when we visit the places they have shot films in, we are always surprised and find it hard to believe the film was shot there. That's because we see a film with a sense of awe and respect. We are subject to the power of storytelling that offers us a location with a reality much different from its true reality. (*A Walk with Kiarostami* 03:01–03:32)

Kiarostami discusses the power of film on people's actual lives. Just as he desired gaps in his storytelling, the question of reality can also be pondered from this elated vantage point. Even if a filmmaker shoots a film on location and does not alter the location, that locality functions in a particular way in the storyline in which it is used. (This idea of how a location is presented on and in a film is explored further in the upcoming section, The Importance of Framing—Reality through and in One's Own Frame.) Two films come to mind that have been repeatedly analyzed by scholars from the perspective of their relation to reality and truth, *Close-Up* (1990) and *Ten* (2002).

To this day, *Close-Up* is one of Kiarostami's works most celebrated by critics and scholars. It is often discussed from the perspective of blurring established genre boundaries. This perspective is popular as Kiarostami retold a true story by restaging it with the actual participants and permission to shoot scenes in court proceedings. Is this film fiction, but based on a true story? Or is it more accurately labeled as nonfiction, featuring reenactments?

Kiarostami has said that "every film is ultimately a reenactment of reality, not that reality itself" (Lopate 39). While the statement was not explicitly made about his film *Close-Up*, interviewer Phillip Lopate asks him about the film immediately following Kiarostami's statement. Kiarostami explains: "[*Close-Up*] was the kind of movie that didn't allow me as a director to manipulate or control it. I feel more like a viewer of that movie than the maker of it." He elaborates that shooting the ending was challenging. After the conclusion of the trial, Sabzian did not want to enter the family's house anymore. "He felt that the kind of authority that had helped him get into the house the first time wasn't there anymore." Kiarostami had to persuade him that this time he brought an actual film crew, something Sabzian had promised them when he was impersonating another filmmaker. In a sense, every reality is created, and categorization has limitations. Labels may not fit. "In my opinion, whether documentary or fiction, it's all one big lie we're telling the viewer. I think our art consists of lying in such a way that the viewer believes it. Which part is documentary and which is made up is all part of the way we work" (*Abbas Kiarostami: Truth and Dreams* 09:07–09:27).[11]

Kiarostami pushed boundaries, exploring what film could be, evolving the form by trying different approaches to storytelling. For Kiarostami, the content of the film and the messages the content sent were the focus in *Close-Up*, and the same applies to *Ten* (2002). For the film *Ten*, he stated in an essay written for the Cannes Film Festival:

> We have a shot in the car with the little boy facing the camera. The scene takes place in the front of the camera. And yet there are also people who pass by, lower their window, and peer into the car. That's documentary. That's background. They look at the camera. But what happens in front of the camera isn't documentary because it's guided and controlled in a way. The person in front of the camera manages to forget

its presence, it vanishes for him. Emotion is created in this way, the result of a certain quantity of energy and information that we give and then recover later. It circulates . . . resulting in the complexity of the situation. (qtd. in Rosenbaum and Saeed-Vafa 125)

The planned and staged content are the focus for each of his films, not the label, not the narrative structure. Arguably, focusing on the genre question misses the actual film content, misses realizing what is happening in front of the camera. Kiarostami would take this blurring of boundaries of truth and reality into many more works throughout his career. Toward the end of this book, Arash T. Riahi's "The Ideal Me and the Real Me" commemorates Kiarostami's contribution to the canon of film and the man behind the camera.

Advancing the Art Form That Is Film vs. Working with Established Practices

This section discusses several moments in Kiarostami's filmmaking career where he experimented with the filmmaking medium. In a 1997 interview, Kiarostami posited, "It's not conscious, but now that one can see all my films as a body of work it seems that they all talk about the same things. Someone once said that every filmmaker basically makes only one film in his lifetime, but he cuts it down and offers it in cinematic installments to his audience over a period of time" (Rice 2). While we may see a through line across someone's body of work, arguably, Kiarostami's films also show an evolving signature. Just as a human's handwriting changes over the course of a lifetime, Kiarostami's work shows evolving penmanship, so to speak. He trials and incorporates techniques that he has wanted to try, thereby not only challenging himself as a filmmaker and artist but also pushing the art form forward and suggesting that *film can be more* than the expected codes and conventions.

One such pushing of boundaries or experimenting was his goal of incorporating seven minutes of black into a film. He had intended to achieve this in *Taste of Cherry* (1997), a film about a protagonist who is contemplating suicide. In the end, Kiarostami did not find a way to organically incorporate this much black into the film. Toward the end of the movie, when the main character Mr. Badii has entered the grave he dug for himself, a storm is passing over him and leaves him in darkness. Lightning strikes illuminate his face occasionally, which permits the viewer to notice that the character has closed his eyes. After the final lightning strike that illuminated Mr. Badii for the audience, we see just under one minute of black while hearing the rain. Then, Kiarostami transitions into the behind-the-scenes footage that concludes the film. In this footage, different people are seen in front of the camera, including soldiers, production crew, and the main actor. This is as close as Kiarostami came to achieving his goal at that time.

While he was unable to achieve the seven minutes of black in *Taste of Cherry*, he eventually accomplished this goal in *ABC Africa* (2001). Due to a storm, a hotel is without power. As the filmmaker and his assistant have to spend the night without power, the darkness is (again) only interrupted by lightning strikes. Here, nature and Kiarostami's idea of telling a story in darkness organically came together. The darkness in the storm and captured on film as black opens up a gap for the audience to fill it with meaning. Does the storm have meaning? Is it coincidental? Do we use the time to reflect on the images shared with us in the minutes leading up to the ominous darkness among the storm? Kiarostami desired to challenge himself to make darkness as meaningful as other visual imagery in a film, and when shooting *ABC Africa* his desire and reality met.

A second way that *ABC Africa* pushed boundaries of filmmaking was during the preproduction process. When Kiarostami agreed to shoot work in Uganda, his plans for the making of the film changed entirely. He visited the people for preproduction research and shot footage with a small digital video camera. Upon his return to Iran, he realized that he had already shot the film. The finished *ABC Africa* consists of footage that was not thought to be in the film. By selecting preproduction footage to become the film (in its entirety), Kiarostami showed again that filmmaking is an art form that can only be planned up to an extent. It is a natural process in which the filmmaker immerses themselves into the project and lets the film become an entity of its own. This process can be organic in the absence of a script, in the absence of being married to a specific order of scenes, characters and their story arcs, and so on.

Over the course of his career, Kiarostami has explained numerous times that he takes notes and has an idea for a film. However, he does not have a detailed shooting script that guides the shooting process. This can be viewed as yet another way he brought a different approach to filmmaking. For him, a film takes shape throughout the production process and in the editing room. This does not mean that he does not create specific dialogue, but his approach is different. As he explained in interviews, he coaches his cast. In summary, the cast does not receive a script with lines they have to memorize. Instead, he speaks with them about the film and other subject matters. What he speaks to them about is intentional on his part though. The next day, when a particular scene is being shot, he may say to an actor to remember the conversation they had the night before and to summarize it. The result is a spontaneous delivery of the content as opposed to a memorized delivery of specific lines. Since Kiarostami mostly worked with nonprofessional actors, this approach resulted in a more authentic delivery of a conversation than a memorized and rehearsed scene would have.[12]

(Related, also important to note is that many of his cast were illiterate.) Miriam Rosen and Abbas Kiarostami chat about the topic in the 1991 interview "The Camera of Art—An Interview with Abbas Kiarostami." Akram Zaatari and Abbas Kiarostami also discuss his approach to writing a script and how it is being used during production in the 1994 interview "Abbas Kiarostami by Akram Zaatari." Both interviews are reprinted in this volume.

Another way Kiarostami evolved in his filmmaking was to bring stories to life by embracing new technologies. *ABC Africa* can be seen as an unintended way of shooting a film on a small camera. The film *Ten* (2002) is one example of deliberately choosing digital cameras to film a feature. The technology used to shoot the film aligned at the right time. In the essay "Auto-Motivations: Digital Cinema and Kiarostami's Relational Aesthetics," Scott Krzych reminds us that the digital camera was essential for the film to be created. He quotes Kiarostami from a 2004 interview that is part of the documentary *10 on Ten* (2004).[13] Without the availability of small digital cameras, the film would have been impossible (Krzych 32). At the time, many filmmakers were holding on to the traditional ways of shooting films with film cameras. Kiarostami incorporated the new technology to bring his vision to life. The film could only be shot with small, digital devices that would permit him and the cameras to fade into the background so his actors could forget that they were being filmed and drive through city streets while immersing themselves in conversations. This permitted their natural performance. (For those readers who are unfamiliar with *Ten* but know James Corden's "Carpool Karaoke," envision a feature film edited together with similar stationary camera shots as used in that program.[14])

By selecting this cinematographic style—a few mounted cameras in a car, as opposed to moving camera shots, and more camera angles—the focus is shifted to the conversations the woman has with her various passengers. The surroundings matter less; the focus is on the happenings inside the car. By utilizing only a few camera angles, audiences know the different camera perspectives a few minutes into the film. The unfamiliar throughout the film is the question of who the next passenger is going to be, and how that person will impact the journey of the female driver (and vice versa). The audience can focus on listening and on understanding and relating to the perspectives the people in the car share with one another and the audience. Especially for Western audiences, the perspectives will likely be dissimilar as the audiences' life experiences are different.

Another aspect of this technique that impacts the outcome is that Kiarostami usually shoots an entire conversation or scene in one take, opting to shoot with two cameras simultaneously to be able to produce invisible cuts and create performance cues by his cast. It permits him to capture the first reactions actors have to the respective scene, as opposed to having experienced it through multiple takes. Over time, any spontaneous, truthful reaction is lost and replaced with a rehearsed response that becomes the character. For instance, *Ten* features a scene in which mother and son yell at one another. Kiarostami was able to capture the surprise of the two actors as they immerse themselves in the confrontation. Kiarostami explained that he rehearsed with them separately, so that neither one knew what the other would say (*Abbas Kiarostami: The Art of Living* 45:10–45:42). This resulted in the surprised reactions on camera when the scene was actually shot. The interaction of his approaches—in this case, limited camera angles, separate rehearsals, and lack of detailed script—leads to the final product, *Ten*.

By shooting the film in this manner, Kiarostami could literally vanish in the backseat during production and only appear when he needed to provide the cast with necessary guidance, like a football coach standing on the sidelines. In a text he wrote for the Cannes Film Festival in 2002, he said: "Sometimes, I tell myself that *TEN* is a film that I could never make again.... Indeed, this is not something that can be repeated easily. It must occur of its own accord, like an incident or a happening" ("Kiarostami on Ten" par. 1). He summarizes a student's reaction to the film style (par. 2), which eventually leads him to this point: "What is at stake [is] the rejection of all elements vital to ordinary cinema. I state, with a great deal of caution, that direction, in the usual sense of the word, can vanish in this kind of process. In this form of cinema, the director is more like a football coach" (par. 4). He continues, "The film was created without being made as such. Even so, it isn't a documentary. Neither a documentary nor a purely fabricated film. Midway between the two perhaps" (par. 5).

For *Shirin* (2008), Kiarostami created again a unique viewing experience for the viewer, unlike anything he had done before. He explores a different method of leaving gaps for the viewer. Viewers of this film watch audience members watch a film. We hear the imaginary film's sound in the film world, but only get to see the responses of cast audience members. This means that the cinema audience (you and I) have to envision what the audience characters in the film may be viewing and why they may have a particular (verbal or nonverbal) response. The viewer is left to imagine a film and what the audience members in the film world think of it. This experience on its own is unique.

However, the production process reveals that the cinema audience that the viewer of *Shirin* sees never even existed. The behind-the-scenes documentary, *Taste of Shirin* (2008), directed by Hamideh Razavi, provides insight into the actual production of the film. Kiarostami invited his cast members for recordings individually or in small groups and told them what to imagine they were seeing on the screen while he filmed their facial expressions. In the documentary, we see Kiarostami work with one of his cast members. He explains to her that he has "portraits of eighty to ninety women, while they are being themselves.

No one's around them; no one's looking at them; they are watching the screen" (01:56–02:08). This is reminiscent of the darkened movie theater. While people are around us, we feel as though we are alone. We have privacy. The darkness means others cannot see my facial expressions, the tears I am shedding for the main protagonist. Kiarostami continues, "in fact, you are all looking at yourselves. Now, as spectators you are looking at yourselves as actors." The actress with which he is shooting asks about what she is imagining watching: "There's nothing funny in it?" Kiarostami confirms, then adds: "However, there exists some kind of fun in life. Wise people know that all this happiness is temporary. As Buddha once said, life is filled with sufferings. The bottom line is we all know that all these joys won't last long, so we don't react promptly to these short-term pleasures." The woman's makeup is applied and the shooting of the scene begins.... We see a shot of the actress, now teary eyed, before cutting to other cast members during production. A montage of women with varying facial expressions is provided (02:09–03:29). This section of *Taste of Shirin* showcases the type of direction Kiarostami provided his cast with. Just as the final film provided gaps for the viewer, his cast was given abstract directions and tasked with making those directions their own in their performances.

In the scene thereafter, we see a hand-drawn image, similar to a storyboard visual, affixed to what appears to be a stand and positioned in front of the cast member. It shows two stick figures with numerous arrows. I—the editor of this book—interpret the visual as the person on the left walking to the person on the right. Kiarostami says to his female cast member, "Just keep staring at this cardboard, as if you are watching a movie on TV. Here is the actor and here is the actress. [*He points to the stick figures*] These arrows show the path. Look at either the woman or the man. Pause on each image for a few seconds, then follow the arrows." Kiarostami looks at the image his camera captures of the woman (and secondary moviegoers situated behind her in the setting). The camera is positioned just below the cardboard. He continues, "Right, your eye movement is great; everything is perfect. The camera is rolling." A crew member holds up a reflector and moves it so that different lighting patterns fall onto the actress's face, just as a screen illuminates us differently based on what is on the screen. Kiarostami's directions continue: "Look at the right of the cardboard, the one looking like a man. [*Time passes*] Now, move your eyes to the left. [*Time passes*] Move back to the right. Now look at the woman" (03:30–04:22). His directions continue in a similar way as we see other cast members sitting in the chairs in front of the camera. A shooting montage follows.

Kiarostami's directions were precise regarding the eye movement, to ensure that he could edit different viewers together. He needed similar eye movements to suggest to the audience of *Shirin* that all these people were really watching the same film simultaneously. Besides that, his directions were void of other cues, leaving it to the performers to decide how to approach this man and woman on the cardboard. Are they happy they are meeting up? Do they wish this hadn't happened? Are they dreading their anticipated interaction (for whatever imagined reason)? Kiarostami appeared to work on the principle of similarity and difference, resembling a cinema audience. Audience members desire to watch the movie; otherwise, they would not have come to the cinema. Yet their responses to a film will vary.

One cast member does ask whether she should imagine sitting in a movie theater. He confirms this and elaborates, "We'll be shooting for five minutes, as if you are watching a ninety-minute movie. It is up to you to define the movie for yourself" (05:20–05:35). As at least some of Kiarostami's directions are improvised, responses to cast members' questions, the directions, and amounts of details vary. To one woman, he says, "First you look but you are not watching," suggesting her character is not yet engaged in the film (05:36–05:39). He adds, "The result will be better if you ignore the camera and imagine yourself alone in the dark," demonstrating his directorial sensibilities of giving respectful guidance to receive the best-possible performance from the cast (05:44–05:49). He suggests that the film is without a director; that it is a situation of "just you and yourself" (05:53–05:57). He jokes with the cast and returns to giving more direction.

Due to his filmmaking approach for this work, the casting for this film also stands apart from that of other films. For this work, he mostly used professional actors. (This will likely not be apparent for foreign audiences, as they are unfamiliar with Iranian actors. They will likely spot Juliette Binoche as "the foreigner" in the theater, recognizing her as a Westerner and professional actress.) Professional actors are familiar with the business of movie making. They know what editing entails, how different shots can be juxtaposed with one another to create the illusion of something the director is aiming for. "Try to have as little expression as possible. It will make our editing job much easier. Otherwise for each expression you might have, we may have to create an incident in the movie that we don't know what it is yet" (06:10–06:25). He would then have to match other people's facial expressions to make it appear they are also watching that incident that was triggered only by the facial expression of one of his cast. It would also limit the options he had, creating the storyline the cast is supposedly watching. "Expression of indifference better fits in our movie," he adds (06:26–6:29).

Of course, he also needs some expressions of joy and other emotions. One way to illicit emotions is with directions. One such direction he provides is: "Rain drops on roses and whiskers on kittens, bright copper kettles and warm woolen mittens, brown paper packages, tied up with strings and so on." The actress smiles and even giggles a little (08:13–08:24). Kiarostami just quoted part of the lyrics of "My Favorite Things" from *The Sound of Music* (1965). He catches his cast member off guard and elicits her reaction to the lyrics. The woman's nonverbal response suggests recognition and some fondness toward the song. Maybe she remembers watching this film for the first time herself. Later on, when he asks, "What are the three fastest ways of communication?" Kiarostami appears to be philosophical. Eventually he adds, "Telephone, television, tell a woman." His cast smiles. Kiarostami used a humorous approach to provoke a response. He adds, "Let your eyes smile, not your lips" (08:32–08:55).

At one point, Kiarostami throws an object to the ground; instinctively, the cast responds with nonverbal responses, such as a little hop or closing of the eyes, but keep performing their role as audience members in a cinema (13:07–13:25). Kiarostami created and captured a performance that can be used in innumerable ways when assembling the final film. What did the fictitious audience supposedly respond to? What made them hop or close their eyes in their seats? Their performance cues give guided creativity back to Kiarostami to determine the answer to that question during the postproduction process.[15]

In a 2000 article in *The Guardian*, Kiarostami is quoted that his "aim is to create a cinema to see how much we can do without actually showing it. How much use we can make of the imagination of the spectator" (Lennon par. 11).[16] Since Kiarostami used these performances to make it appear as though all these audience members were watching the same film in a movie theater, he appropriated their performances for another narrative. During production, he was focused on creating generic footage that could be shaped into a narrative that he was yet creating.[17]

(Besides giving direction to his cast, Kiarostami also gives his crew directions, such as lighting being changed to be "more playful and visible in the background" [06:51–06:59]. Besides a crew member with the reflector, a second crew member was holding up boards with different cutouts to give the illusion of changing light patterns falling on the cast of audience members. This was necessary to support the illusion for us, the audience of *Shirin*, that the people we see on screen were sitting in front of a cinema screen, watching a film.)

Kiarostami pushed the art form of cinema in his approach to shooting *Shirin*, suggesting one's imagination can be as powerful, if not more powerful, when one can only watch a movie secondhand, via the facial expressions of others. The audience is left to decide what the topics of this film are—is it being fooled? It is living through someone else? Is it another approach to the question of truth? What is truth? And, related, what is a fact? Kiarostami left the gap wide open. The interview "*Shirin* as Described by Kiarostami" provides the reader of this book with a closer look at the final product.

When making what would become his final film, *24 Frames* (2017), Kiarostami's health had created limitations that altered his creative process and approach to filmmaking. The film was created in front of a computer, not out in nature. Still images were animated; this animation process suggested what film could be. Readers may think that animated images already exist, thinking of computer-generated imagery (CGI) films, such as James Cameron's *Avatar* (2009) or Disney's *Frozen* (2013). Kiarostami's animation process was very different, as was the narrative content and the film's structure. He had made the animation process his own.

24 Frames—which was completed by his son, Ahmad Kiarostami, and premiered posthumously at the Cannes Film Festival in May 2017—invited the audience on a journey into experimental cinema. We are asked to open ourselves up to what twenty-four (still) film frames can capture. On its own, every frame is a still image. But when we imagine what may have happened just before or after a still image was taken, motion is revealed. Life is revealed that we otherwise likely would have overlooked. Kiarostami's final contribution to film art was described as many things by critics, including being a "haunted ghost-film" that "demands patience and engagement" (Brooks par. 3). He showcased one more time that for him cinema does not equal storytelling.

The film opens to the visual of what appears to be a painting. Eventually, aspects in the painting, such as the chimney smoke, begin to move. Life begins. Each of the frames references other forms of art, among them photography, beginning each frame with a still image that lets the viewer ponder what may happen, before the visual animates and shares a moment of life before the frame concludes again. Similar to a room in which works of art have been arranged along a wall and a visitor views them in the order in which they are displayed, Kiarostami provides us with twenty-four images in an order chosen by him. He provides us with the black space in between each image, the equivalent of walking to the next work situated along the gallery wall, to reflect, to make meaning, to let our minds wander. Unlike in a museum, a cinema audience cannot skip a work of art, unless we step outside the theater. The order of each frame as well as its length has been chosen for us by the filmmaker. The interaction between the image and the viewer is controlled by the viewer. While this book focuses on his film work, at this time it makes sense to remember that Kiarostami also produced installations for museums. This film was created after he had produced work for different outlets in the art domain. (For example, for a discussion of his work outside the film domain, Jenny Chamarette's "Transnational Borders and Intermedial Spectacle: Kiarostami and Opera, between France and Iran" contextualizes three different works by Kiarostami—one installation, one feature film, and one opera—from the perspective of transcultural productions. See the additional resources for a complete citation.) To him, poetry and film can also intertwine and enhance one another: "When I talk about poetic cinema, I am thinking about the kind of cinema that possesses the qualities of poetry, that encompasses the vast potential of poetry. It has the capabilities of a prism. It has a complexity to it. It has a lasting quality. It's like an unfinished puzzle that invites us to decipher the message and put the pieces together in whatever arrangement we want" (*Lessons* 20). In this book, the interview "Nature Has No Culture: The Photographs of Abbas Kiarostami" provides the reader with a look at Kiarostami's photography work.

Overall, several of the interviews in this volume discuss production processes and Kiarostami's decisions on how to create a film. For example, Kiarostami speaks about several of his films, including *The Wind Will Carry Us* (1999) and *ABC Africa*, in the 2003 interview for *Revolver*. Reading about the behind-the-scenes footage of *Shirin* may also be especially inspirational for anyone studying and/or practicing filmmaking. Kiarostami is giving a master class on make-believe that anyone can try to replicate to realize how difficult it is and how much planning and attention to detail has to be ensured to be able to have this illusion become successful in postproduction and, eventually, in the real cinema, when real audiences watch the finished product. The film had a small budget. Yes, it required the skill of professional actors. On the other hand, it was shot in a living room with minimal set needs and production equipment. Students often feel that the lack of budget limits what they can accomplish. Kiarostami illustrates otherwise. Having only a small budget furthers creativity. How does one create the illusion of a space without building the space or even shooting it in an existing space of that kind? How does one create the illusion of characters engaging in a behavior (in this case, watching a film in a cinema) when that is not what they are doing? If you are now intrigued, the coda in this book includes a zero-budget challenge to practice the art and craft of filmmaking, provided by Kiarostami himself.

The Importance of Framing—
Reality through and in One's Own Frame

No one sees the world in an identical way to someone else. The way a shot is framed and reveals information to a viewer is one key element of the film medium. As Kiarostami is also known as a photographer, the framing of a shot itself holds enormous importance to the way he creates and shares work with his audiences. "For me, the camera is exactly the same as a pen. It can be used by the common person or it can be used by Baudelaire to create a great poem" (*Abbas Kiarostami: The Art of Living* 00:49–01:02).[18]

In *A Walk with Kiarostami* (2001), Kiarostami and Akrami had visited one of the islands on which Robert Flaherty had shot the film *Man of Aran* (1934). Kiarostami remarks: "That's why I think the island we visited was exactly the same island but it did not look anything like the island Flaherty used, because we didn't see it from his point of view" (03:38–03:49). In 1978, James Brown and George Stoney codirected *How the Myth Was Made: A Study of Robert Flaherty's "Man of Aran."* The storyline on IMDb includes that the documentary directors conclude that the film was not a documentary in the expected sense of the genre. Instead, it was "Flaherty's personal and romantic vision of how life should be lived" and not how the residents lived ("Plot" par. 1). This illustrates what Kiarostami referred to as Flaherty's viewpoint. When we like a film, we want the location to keep the film's reality, yet that reality never existed in the first place. Kiarostami elaborates, "We are no longer under [Flaherty's] viewing conditions. He showed us the island through his own frame. But left on our own, we tend to look around freely, and are virtually lacking the kind of concentration we always have in a movie theater. While encountering reality, we are not concentrating, and we are not guided. That's why we roam around and fail to see what we need to see" (*A Walk with Kiarostami* 03:50–04:13).

On one hand, looking around freely means we get to experience the reality of the location filtered by our own eyes and brain. No one suggests to us where to look and what is important. It is up to us to make that decision, including deciding that nothing may be of importance. On the other hand, if we don't make a decision, then we will have missed seeing what we could have seen. A filmmaker makes a decision for us. When they select a location, they decide how it should be framed in the shot, how it should be (re)presented on the screen. It is this choice that engrains itself in the audience's mind. That particular frame, that particular light—that is what the reality of the locality is. Should it not match when we visit, then we find ourselves off balance.

Kiarostami adds that the most important aspect of creating reality is in the way it is framed (*A Walk with Kiarostami* 04:46–04:49). He continues,

> I take a picture, and I wonder whether I should print it or not. I keep hesitating, but I print it anyway. Now, the minute I place the picture in a white passe-par-tout frame, all of a sudden it becomes more attractive, and when I frame it and look at it behind the glass, it looks perfectly acceptable. So, I think the idea of framing a subject in a picture is as important as its content. By choosing and framing something, you are giving it a measure of importance, resulting from your selection. As soon as you select something, you give it an additional value that separates it from anything else. (04:50–05:37)

The documentary's observational mode shows some of Kiarostami's process. At one point, the path Kiarostami, Akrami, and crew had been walking on features a junction that leads to a gated field. Kiarostami chooses to walk the little section of dirt road that leads to the gate instead of continuing to walk on the main path. He takes pictures, capturing the gated field and sky. He provides insight into his framing of earth and sky; he selects the ratio based on what he feels should be dominant in the image (08:24–09:22). Throughout the piece, viewers see Kiarostami take pictures with his own camera. At one point, Kiarostami happily utters, "I am about to take a really nice picture, finally" (10:32–10:36). We are left to realize how much time it takes him to get the frames he feels are good and that we get to see. Many more pictures have been taken that don't make the cut and audiences never get to see. Watching Kiarostami look at his surroundings, lift up the camera, and frame shots—most of the time we can only imagine based on the shot we see what he is framing and how he is framing it—possibly tells us much more about the artist than his verbal answers. He sees the world in his unique perspective, picks up on details that we may have seen not at all or in a different way. For Kiarostami, "Photography is more of an original and potent art form compared to cinema because cinema has radically shifted from being a pure art form because it has to tell a story" (*Abbas Kiarostami: The Art of Living* 38:40–38:52).

While Akrami does point out that he seems to favor framing individual objects, such as a lone tree, Kiarostami explains that he is unsure whether that is due to aesthetics or concept (*A Walk with Kiarostami* 28:50–29:10). He implies that one should not read too much into patterns. Framing choices might be explainable by mundane reasons. Eventually, he exemplifies, "A single tree is more of a tree than a number of them" (29:12–29:18). He summarizes a story that is known in in the US as the saying that one can't see the forest for all its trees. "When you have a lot of trees lined up next to each other, you don't see trees anymore. You see something else that carries a different concept" (29:19–29:49).

We can wonder what (concept) Kiarostami saw when he created the six-minute segment known as "Rug," which is also known as "Is There a Place to Approach?" It is part of the feature film *Persian Carpet* (2007). (The film is made up of various shorts created by several directors.) Depending on the segment's title—"Rug" or "Is There a Place to Approach?"—one's reading position will likely be different. His segment is made up of one extreme close-up (XCU) long take. It permits the viewer to take time to study the object—a rug—and realize details in the object that we otherwise likely never would notice. Through its approach (in particular, its framing and editing pace), the film may appear to ask the viewer to really pay attention and take in what is present in front of us and to realize its value. The reactions are those of each individual viewer and are each as valid as the next. Will I respond with appreciation for the intricacies of the rug? Or with boredom? With awe for the craftsmanship that results in such a rug? Or with indifference? Will it inspire me to take moments of pause in my own life to really pay attention and shift my focus completely onto whatever caught my interest? Or will I continue to live my life, rushing from one appointment to the next? In contrast, when considering the latter title—the question "Is There a Place to Approach?"—I may look at the object, studying it with the goal in mind to answer the question. From that reading position, the rug looks different, even though it is exactly the same object as it was before. The question suggests a different viewing experience and an altered framing concept.

Generally, a created image—whether "Rug" or another piece of work—represents the creator's vision of reality of whatever they captured and in whichever medium it was captured in. Akrami posits, "What is particularly noticeable in the framing of your films is how the edges of the frames don't constitute an end. There are always signifiers in the middle or on the edges of the frames that point to things beyond the frames" (13:03–13:24). This is part of his meaning-making of Kiarostami's vision. It's a way of labeling and identifying one person's work. Kiarostami agrees that that is part of his framing and, for him, represents "continuity" (13:26). What the words means to him specifically in this context is left open to the viewer's interpretation.

Readers interested in the concept of framing may find the following interviews reprinted in this book of particular interest: Peter Rist's "Meeting Abbas Kiarostami—The 24th Montreal World Film Festival" addresses the topic by discussing how a location is revealed to the viewer by framing it through car windows, at the beginning of *And Life Goes On* (1992). Similarly, in "Interview with Abbas Kiarostami for a book by Jonathan Rosenbaum," Rosenbaum concludes the conversation with raising the way Kiarostami frames shots through car windows. Kiarostami replies that the windows of the car became his frames as he was driving his car. Framing can also be pondered from the perspective of inclusion versus exclusion in "A Fax Conversation between Jonathan Rosenbaum and Abbas Kiarostami." The asynchronous conversation illuminates a critic's response to the ending of *Taste of Cherry* (1997). It illustrates the power of a film's ending on the audience, and the power said audience has on a film's exhibition. In Khatereh Khodaei's "*Shirin* as Described by Kiarostami," framing is also considered from the vantage point of inclusion versus exclusion. Again, for a discussion of Kiarostami's photography work, readers may find "Nature Has No Culture: The Photographs of Abbas Kiarostami" by Shiva Balaghi and Anthony Shadid of particular interest.

Closing Words

Jean-Luc Godard has said: "Film begins with D. W. Griffith and ends with Abbas Kiarostami." According to Martin Scorsese: "Kiarostami represents the highest level of artistry in the cinema." When these words are quoted at Kiarostami, he winces most charmingly. "This admiration is perhaps most appropriate after I am dead," he says. (Jeffries par. 4)

These quotes illustrate the status that had been bestowed on Kiarostami and that framed articles on him and about his work. It is hoped that reading the interviews in this volume along with other summaries of works—such as articles and documentary shorts mentioned in this introduction—provides readers the possibility to paint their own picture of Kiarostami. Jamsheed Akrami points to Kiarostami's success and wonders whether he has reached his goal. Kiarostami responds:

If we set a goal for ourselves to reach, like someone whose goal is to reach a mountain top, then you can relax when you achieve your goal. But if you didn't set a goal for yourself in the first place, naturally you cannot be thinking in terms of achieving a goal. You cannot think that you have arrived now! You haven't arrived anywhere, because it's only in the course of planning something that you may reach somewhere. Without planning, you don't reach anywhere. It's like breathing. You never think you have breathed enough. If you think of beathing as a necessity, not a goal, then you don't think in terms of realizing a goal. (*A Walk with Kiarostami* 20:46–21:33)

In *A Walk with Kiarostami*, Kiarostami, Akrami, and crew walk back the way they came. Kiarostami points out that while they are walking the same path, the light has changed, and so have they. "There is an often-quoted saying that nobody can claim he has swum in the same river twice, since neither the river nor the person would remain the same. Every time he swims, he is a new person in a new river" (22:02–22:36).

Love is like a plant. There's a hidden part we can't see until it emerges from the soil. So we can't say love is born the moment we first see it. What about its roots? Its roots are invisible but also undeniable. We can't deny their existence. Love happens inside a person until it reaches a level where it's expressed. And declaring one's love is one of the most common and appropriate ways to express it.[19] (*Abbas Kiarostami: Truth and Dreams* 28:00–28:38)

I would like to thank Dr. Gerald Peary for the opportunity to edit this volume. I would also like to send my sincere gratitude to Emily Snyder Bandy, associate editor at the University Press of Mississippi, for guiding me through the entire process. A very special thanks to Frank Cooper, JD, Dr. Micky Lee, and Dr. Patricia Reeve for their continued support throughout this project. Also, a very special thanks to my focus group audience who took the time to watch a Kiarostami film and answer questions. Unfortunately, this portion of the introduction became literally the last piece that ended up on the "cutting room floor." Although the data is not directly discussed in this introduction anymore, the responses by the participants have influenced several subsections of this introduction. Thank you for being part of the focus group! Given the already-mentioned pandemic context, I would also like to send a special thank you to all the journal and magazine editors and authors who assisted me in contacting interviewers for permission requests. Last but certainly not least, I would like to thank Anita Sen for her invaluable clerical support.

MR

Notes

1. In particular, the book *Abbas Kiarostami Interviews*, published in 2020 and edited by Presley Parks, Paul Cronin, and Michel Ciment, provides a large collection of interviews of the filmmaker.
2. Kiarostami's text written for the one-hundred-year anniversary of cinema is available on numerous websites, including https://www.sabzian.be/article/an-unfinished-cinema.
3. The name of the protagonist, Mr. Badii, was spelled "Mr. Badie" throughout the entire article. It has been amended for consistency in this introduction.
4. At the time when timestamps for in-text citations were added to this text, the documentary had become temporarily unavailable to me. It is a special feature on the *Shirin* DVD. My apologies for any inconvenience.
5. The film is available as an additional feature on the DVD *Close-Up*, distributed by the Criterion Collection.
6. At the time when timestamps for in-text citations were added to this text, the interview had become temporarily unavailable to me. My apologies for any inconvenience. The interview is a special feature on the *Taste of Cherry* DVD, distributed by the Criterion Collection.
7. At the time when timestamps for in-text citations were added to this text, the interview had become temporarily unavailable to me. My apologies for any inconvenience. The interview is a special feature on the *Taste of Cherry* DVD, distributed by the Criterion Collection.
8. As discussed earlier, Kiarostami began his filmmaking while he was working for the Institute for the Intellectual Development of Children and Young Adults. Eventually, he left the institute. However, this was not Kiarostami's choice. Jeffries's article illuminates that after *Homework* (1989)—a film that required changes and was banned for three years nonetheless—Kiarostami explained that he "was forced to leave Kanun because they disagreed with the film" (par. 18).

9. At the time when timestamps for in-text citations were added to this text, the interview had become temporarily unavailable to me. My apologies for any inconvenience. The interview is a special feature on the *Taste of Cherry* DVD, distributed by the Criterion Collection.
10. Kiarostami is regularly referred to as the auteur of the 1990s. Spanish filmmaker auteur Pedro Almodóvar was particularly celebrated in the 2000s, with his films *Talk to Her* (2002) and *Volver* (2006).
11. Kiarostami also speaks about this issue in Godfrey Cheshire's book *Conversations with Kiarostami*, listed in the appendix.
12. Due to taking a different approach to filmmaking and working with nonprofessional actors, the opening of *Through the Olive Trees* (1994) may give viewers an idea into his casting process. The film opens with the casting of a female lead at a girls' school in rural Iran. The fictional director speaks to the camera, providing context as to their location and purpose. The female students are lined up and the director walks through the lines. He asks some of them their names. When he reaches Tahareh, he asks his production assistant to note down her address. He also asks other female students to provide their addresses. One student asks what the point of all of this is since they never will see the film. Absent in this entire casting was the reading of a scene to determine "suitability" for the specific role that one may associate with casting for a Hollywood film. Instead, the director seems to make the decision based on his experience and intuition, with the audience wondering what he is looking for, what this female role may be. Kiarostami leaves a gap for the viewer. Eventually, as the film unfolds, we see who the character is that he was casting for, and whatever our expectations may have been, we shift our idea of the character to what is presented to us.
13. *10 on Ten* (2004) is a documentary directed by Abbas Kiarostami in which he reflects on his own filmmaking techniques.
14. "Carpool Karaoke" is a segment in *The Late Late Show with James Corden*. The first episode aired in 2015. It now also exists as a standalone, "Carpool Karaoke: The Series."
15. When the first part of *Taste of Shirin* concludes, the documentary shows the audio recording process. Actors are in a recording studio, reading from a script. This is the film the cast is supposedly watching. Unlike his other films, a script is essential for this part of the film.
16. One may connect this comment also to his desire for a prolonged period of black, discussed earlier in this section.
17. The seven minutes of black goal can also be viewed as another approach of creating a cinema-without-explicitly-showing-action.
18. Charles Baudelaire (1821–1867) was a French poet. His most famous work was *Les Fleurs du Mal* (*The Flowers of Evil*), published in 1857.
19. Kiarostami's final music choice, his coda in *24 Frames*, was Andrew Lloyd Webber's ballade *Love Never Dies*. Watching the film in the darkened cinema, I was reminded of Kiarostami saying that "the start and end of a film are always arbitrary. We close to cut a section like a tape that is unwinding" (*Making of "Like Someone in Love"*). His final music choice had me make two connections: First, referring to the song's title, just as Kiarostami's love for the cinema never wavered, his legacy on the film medium will remain forever. Viewers of his films will continue to feel his passion—his love—for the medium. Second, while

he has said that he does not like to elicit emotions in audiences, *Love Never Dies* permitted audiences a moment to be emotional and to find some closure—if they so wish—knowing this would be the last time that a new work of this great filmmaker had revealed itself on the big screen.

Works Cited

Abbas Kiarostami: The Art of Living. Directed by P. Collins and F. Daly, A Harvest Films Production, 2003. *Vimeo*, uploaded by Experimental Film Society, 5 Jul. 2016, vimeo.com/173519394.

Abbas Kiarostami: Truth and Dreams. Directed by Jean-Pierre Limosin, 1994.

ABC Africa. Directed by Abbas Kiarostami. New Yorker Films, 2001.

And Life Goes On. Directed by Abbas Kiarostami. The Criterion Collection, 1991.

Aufderheide, Pat. "Real Life Is More Important Than Cinema." *Cineaste*, vol. 21, no. 3, 1995, pp. 31–33.

Avatar. Directed by James Cameron. 20th Centry Fox, 2009.

"BFI Fellows." *BFI*, www.bfi.org.uk/strategy-policy/bfi-fellows. Accessed 26 Nov. 2021.

Bread and Alley. Directed by Abbas Kiarostami. 1970.

Brooks, Xan. "24 Frames Review—A Mesmeric Glimpse into Abbas Kiarostami's Mysterious Mind." *The Guardian*, 23 May 2017, www.theguardian.com/film/2017/may/23/24-frames-review-abbas-kiarostami. Accessed 26 Nov. 2021.

"Carpool Karaoke." *The Late Late Show with James Corden*, season 1, CBS, 2015.

Case #1, Case #2. Directed by Abbas Kiarostami. 1979.

Certified Copy. Directed by Abbas Kiarostami. The Criterion Collection, 2010.

Chamarette, Jenny. "Transitional Borders and Intermedial Spectacle: Kiarostami and Opera, between France and Iran." *Studies in French Cinema*, vol. 13, no. 3, 2013, pp. 257–71.

Cheshire, Godfrey. *Conversations with Kiarostami*, edited by Jim Colvill, The Film Desk, 2019.

Cheshire, Godfrey. "In the City of Abbas." *Film Comment*, vol. 53, no. 6, November-December 2017, pp. 52–57.

Close-Up. Directed by Abbas Kiarostami. The Criterion Collection, 1990.

Five Dedicated to Ozu. Directed by Abbas Kiarostami. 2003.

Frozen. Directed by Chris Buck and Jennifer Lee. Walt Disney Studios Home Entertainment, 2013.

Homework. Directed by Abbas Kiarostami. The Criterion Collection, 1989.

Interview from 1997 with Abbas Kiarostami, conducted by Film Scholar Jamsheed Akrami. Directed by Jamsheed Akrami. The Criterion Collection, 1997.

"Is There a Place to Approach?" Directed by Abbas Kiarostami. *Persian Carpet*, 2007.

Jeffries, Stuart. "Landscapes of the Mind." *The Guardian*, 16 Apr. 2005, www.theguardian.com/film/2005/apr/16/art. Accessed 26 Nov. 2021.

Kiarostami, Abbas. "Kiarostami on Ten." *Ten* Press Kit, Zeitgeist Films, 2002, zeitgeistfilms.com/media/films/89/presskit.pdf. Accessed 26 Nov. 2021.

Kiarostami, Abbas. "An Unfinished Cinema," *Sabzian*, 15 May 2019, www.sabzian.be/article/an-unfinished-cinema. Accessed 26 Nov. 2021.

Lennon, Peter. "One of Your Scenes Is Missing." *The Guardian*, 14 Sep. 2000, www.theguardian.com/film/2000/sep/15/culture.features1. Accessed 26 Nov. 2021.

Lessons with Kiarostami, edited by Paul Cronin. Sticking Place Books, 2015.

Like Someone in Love. Directed by Abbas Kiarostami. The Criterion Collection, 2012.

Lloyd Webber, Andrew. "Love Never Dies." *Love Never Dies*, Verve, 2010.

Lopate, Phillip. "Kiarostami Close Up." *Film Comment*, vol. 32, no. 4, Jul.-Aug. 1996, pp. 37–40.

Knox, Jim. "Cacti Blossom in a Desert: Some Short Films of Abbas Kiarostami." *Senses of Cinema*, no. 29, December 2003, www.sensesofcinema.com/2003/abbas-kiarostami/kiarostami_shorts/. Accessed 26 Nov. 2021.

Krzych, Scott. "Auto-Motivations: Digital Cinema and Kiarostami's Relational Aesthetics." *The Velvet Light Trap*, no. 66, Fall 2010, pp. 26–35.

Mahdi, Ali Akbar. "In Dialogue with Kiarostami," *The Iranian*, 25 Aug. 1998. www.iranian.com/Arts/Aug98/Kiarostami/. Accessed 26 Nov. 2021.

Making of "Like Someone in Love." Directed by Morteza Farshbaf. The Criterion Collection, 2012.

Man of Aran. Directed by Robert Flaherty. The Criterion Collection, 1934.

Palmer, Landon. "6 Filmmaking Tips from Abbas Kiarostami." 18 Apr. 2014, filmschoolrejects.com/6-filmmaking-tips-from-abbas-kiarostami-6a30890e68c7/. Accessed 26 Nov. 2021.

"Plot—How the Myth Was Made: A Study of Robert Flaherty's Man of Aran." IMDb.com, www.imdb.com/title/tt1852805/plotsummary?ref_=tt_ov_pl. Accessed 26. Nov. 2021.

"Repérages." *A Propos de Nice, La Suite*. Directed by Abbas Kiarostami. 1995.

The Report. Directed by Abbas Kiarostami. The Criterion Collection, 1977.

Rice, Julian. *Abbas Kiarostami's Cinema of Life: From "Homework" to "Like Someone in Love."* Rowman & Littlefield Publishers, 2020.

Roads of Kiarostami. Directed by Abbas Kiarostami. 2005.

Rosenbaum, Jonathan, and Mehrnaz Saeed-Vafa. *Abbas Kiarostami: Expanded Second Edition (Contemporary Film Directors)*. University of Illinois Press, 2018.

Shirin. Directed by Abbas Kiarostami. 2008.

So Can I. Directed by Abbas Kiarostami. 1975.

Sterritt, David. "The Element of Chance." *Film Comment*, vol. 52, no. 5, September–October 2016, pp. 94–95.

Taste of Cherry. Directed by Abbas Kiarostami. The Criterion Collection, 1997.

Taste of Shirin. Directed by Hamideh Razavi, 2008. *YouTube*, uploaded by Sayantan Dutta, 20 Jun. 2020, www.youtube.com/watch?v=IkeBDYryepk.

Ten. Directed by Abbas Kiarostami. 2002.

10 on Ten. Directed by Abbas Kiarostami. 2004.

Tickets. Directed by Abbas Kiarostami, Ken Loach, and Ermanno Olmi. (2005)

The Traveler. Directed by Abbas Kiarostami. The Criterion Collection, 1974.

24 Frames. Directed by Abbas Kiarostami. The Criterion Collection, 2017.

Two Solutions for One Problem. Directed by Abbas Kiarostami. 1975.

A Walk with Kiarostami. Directed by Jamsheed Akrami, 2001. *YouTube*, uploaded by lachambreverte, 18 Feb. 2018, www.youtube.com/watch?v=KKoSoL_jIWE.

A Week with Kiarostami. Directed by Yuji Mohara, 1999. *YouTube*, uploaded by Sayantan Dutta, 11 Jun. 2020, www.youtube.com/watch?v=0-U3xFmPqUs (Part 1).

A Week with Kiarostami. Directed by Yuji Mohara, 1999. *YouTube*, uploaded by Sayantan Dutta, 11 Jun. 2020, www.youtube.com/watch?v=u9CTskB_Bhc (Part 2).

Where's the Friend's House? Directed by Abbas Kiarostami. The Criterion Collection, 1987.

The Wind Will Carry Us. Directed by Abbas Kiarostami. New Yorker Films Video, 2002.

Zavattini, Cesare. "Some Ideas on the Cinema." *Film: A Montage of Theories*, edited by Richard D. MacCann, 1966.

Chronology

1940	Born June 22, 1940, in Tehran, Iran.
1958	Begins his studies at University of Tehran's College of Fine Arts; he majors in painting and graphic design.
1960s	Graduates with a BA in fine arts. After the conclusion of his studies, he illustrates children's books, creates TV commercials, and designs credit sequences for films.
1969	Invited to create a filmmaking division for the Institute for the Intellectual Development of Children and Young Adults (elsewhere, its name appears as Kanun Parvaresh Fekri).
1969	Marries Parvin Amir-Gholi.
1970	*Bread and Alley*, the first short film created in the filmmaking division of Kanun Parvaresh Fekri, is completed and screened. It is awarded the Jury Special Award at the 5th Tehran International Festival of Films for Children and Young Adults.
1970s	More short films produced by Kanun Parvaresh Fekri follow, among others *Recess*, *The Experience*, *So Can I*, *Two Solutions for One Problem*, *The Colors*, and *Case #1, Case #2*. Kiarostami is credited for both screenplay and directing for all of them and receives editing credit for some of them.
1971	First son, Ahmad, is born.
1974	Kiarostami makes his directorial narrative feature debut with *The Traveler*, also made under the auspices of Kanun Parvaresh Fekri. It is awarded the Jury's Grand Prize at the 9th Tehran International Festival of Films for Children and Young Adults.
1974	He also directs *The Experience*. It is awarded the 1st Prize in the narrative category at the 4th Giffoni International Film Festival, Italy.
1976	*Two Solutions for One Problem* wins the 1st Prize at the International Educational Festival in Mexico.
1977	He shoots his first independent film, *The Report*, about a marriage breaking down.
1978	His second child, son Bahman, is born.
1978–79	The Iranian Revolution takes place.

1980s	Throughout the decade, Abbas Kiarostami's films receive awards at Iranian film festivals.
1982	Divorce from his wife, Parvin Amir-Gholi.
1984	He shoots his first documentary, *First Graders*. By this time, he has directed a total of eighteen films for Kanun Parvaresh Fekri.
1987	He makes the film *Where's the Friend's House?* which will eventually become known as the first installment in the Koker trilogy.
1989	He directs his second documentary, *Homework*.
1989	*Where's the Friend's House?* is awarded the Bronze Leopard at the 42nd Locarno International Film Festival. The film receives four additional honors at the festival.
1990	*Where's the Friend's House?* is awarded the Best Film Award at the International Film Festival of the Royal Film Archive of Belgium.
1990	*Close-Up* is the first film to blur the lines between documentary and fiction, and is the first movie to take a reflexive perspective on cinema itself and in relation to the subjects it documents. The film is an award recipient at the 3rd Rimini International Film Festival, Italy, and also receives the Prize of the Quebec Critics Association at the 19th Montreal International Festival of New Cinema & Video, Canada. At the 5th Dunkerque International Film Festival, France, Kiarostami is awarded the Best Director Prize for the film.
1990s	Abbas Kiarostami receives many awards and other recognitions for his work across Europe, North and South America, and Australia. (Only the most prestigious recognitions will be listed separately in this chronology.)
1992	*And Life Goes On*, the film known as the second part of the Koker trilogy and also known under the title *Life and Nothing More*, is released. It is awarded the Best Film Award of Un Certain Regard at the 45th Cannes International Film Festival, France. Un Certain Regard is a section showcasing films with unusual styles or storytelling approaches. At the festival, Kiarostami also receives the Roberto Rossellini Award for his film career.
1994	The final film in the Koker trilogy, *Through the Olive Trees*, is released.
1995	Kiarostami begins exhibitions of other art at Pinacoteca Casa Rusca, Locarno, Switzerland. (Only some of the exhibits are listed in this chronology.)
1996	He is bestowed with the Officier de la Légion d'honneur from the Ministry of Culture and Art of France.
1997	*Taste of Cherry* is released and awarded the Palme d'Or at the 50th Cannes International Film Festival. Kiarostami also receives the Vittorio de

	Sica Memorial Award for his film career from the Vittorio de Sica Foundation, Italy. UNESCO awards him with the Federico Fellini Gold Medal for his film career.
1999	*The Wind Will Carry Us* is released and awarded the Jury Special Prize at the 56th Venice International Film Festival.
2000s	Kiarostami continues to receive awards and prizes. Throughout the decade, he also exhibits art in galleries and museums across the world, including New York, Turin, Tokyo, Tehran, Sao Paulo, London, Seoul, Belgrade, Istanbul, and Dubai among many more.
2001	*ABC Africa*, a documentary, becomes his first film shot in a foreign country.
2002	*Ten* marks a departure from the previous feature films, by being a low-budget digital film shot in a car.
2003	*Five Dedicated to Ozu* begins a period of work in which Kiarostami avoids narrative storytelling; the film consists of five seashore shots without camera movement.
2004	Kiarostami receives the Japan Art Association's Praemium Imperiale Prize for theater/film.
2005	Kiarostami is awarded a fellowship at the British Film Institute and is appointed president of the jury for the Camera d'Or Award at the Cannes Film Festival.
2007	The Museum of Modern Art and P.S.1 Contemporary Art Center present the largest exhibition of Kiarostami's work in the US, titled "Abbas Kiarostami: Image Maker, a Three-Part Exhibition of Film, Photography, and Installations." As part of the exhibit, *Five Dedicated to Ozu* is presented as a video installation with separate projections.
2008	His feature film *Shirin* is released.
2010	*Certified Copy*, which takes place and was shot in Italy, is released. Juliette Binoche is awarded the Best Actress Award at the 63rd Cannes International Film Festival, France.
2012	His next feature film, *Like Someone in Love*, is shot in Japan. *Sight & Sound* ranks *Close-Up* at number 42 on their list "The 50 Greatest Films of All Time."
2016	What would become the final exhibit of his artwork during his lifetime opens at CerModern in Ankara in January 2016. The exhibit features a selection of his photography and video works.
2016	While in the middle of making the feature film *24 Frames*, Kiarostami has to be hospitalized and undergoes multiple surgeries. Eventually, he is transferred to a hospital in Paris, France.

2016	He dies on July 4, 2016, in Paris, France. According to the Kiarostami Foundation's website, he had been preparing his next film project, to be shot in China. He is buried at Tok Mazra'eh Cemetery in Lavasan, Shemiranat, Iran.
2017	The Writers Guild of America West awards him the Jean Renoir Award for International Screenwriting Achievement posthumously. His son Ahmad accepts the award on his late father's behalf.
2017	Abbas Kiarostami's son Ahmad finishes *24 Frames* after his father's passing. Posthumously, *24 Frames* premieres at the 70th Cannes Film Festival.
2017	mk2 acquires the rights to Kiarostami's first twenty films, all shot for Iran's Institute for the Intellectual Development of Children and Young Adults, also known as Kanun Parvaresh Fekri.
2018	*24 Frames* enjoys a limited release at the Film Society at Lincoln Center in New York City and other cities in the US and worldwide.
2018	BBC Culture's "The 100 Greatest Foreign-Language Films" includes Kiarostami's *Close-Up* (rank 39), *Where's the Friend's House?* (rank 94), and *Taste of Cherry* (rank 97).
2019	Tehran's Golestan Gallery exhibits more than thirty paintings created by Kiarostami. Most of the works were created between 1980 and 2000 and were borrowed from private collectors for the two-week exhibit.
2020	Ahmad Kiarostami files a lawsuit in Iran against the publication of the book *I'm Home*, which features personal letters by Kiarostami to his former wife. The court orders all copies of the book to be removed from bookstores.
2021	The Pompidou Center in Paris along with mk2 announce an exhibition, titled "Where Is Friend Kiarostami?" of Kiarostami's entire works for May 2021.

Filmography

The filmography in this volume presents the best-possible current summary of Kiarostami's work. Unfortunately, inaccuracies are (almost) guaranteed. Due to many Kiarostami films being unavailable, I had to rely on existing sources to determine credit information. This presented challenges. I compared information from various sources. One such source, the Kiarostami Foundation website, is under construction at the time of this writing. Additionally, due to translations from Arabic to Latin alphabet, names are spelled differently, pending translation. To clarify some variations in name listings—such as who the cinematographer was on a given film—when possible, the original closing credit scenes were screened and translated. The question of spelling names in the Latin alphabet still remained. Overall, this filmography represents the best effort to provide a complete summary of Kiarostami's work in regard to his films (including short and long form). Excluded are works that are not (primarily) in the film domain (such as photography and art installations). Due to the contradictions in some translations in regard to crew roles and the spelling of names in particular, I would like to apologize to any person whose name has been misspelled or has been omitted.

BREAD AND ALLEY (1970)
Iran
Production Company: Kanun Parvaresh Fekri
Director: **Abbas Kiarostami**
Screenplay: Taghi Kiarostami
Cinematography: Mehrdad Fakhimi
Editing: Manuchehr Oliai
Music: Paul Desmond
Cast: Reza Hashemi, Mehdi Shahranfar
Black and White, 10 minutes

BREAKTIME / RECESS (1972)
Iran
Production Company: Kanun Parvaresh Fekri

Director: **Abbas Kiarostami**
Screenplay: **Abbas Kiarostami** (based on a story by Masud Madani)
Cinematography: Ali Reza Zarrindast, Morteza Rastegar
Editing: **Abbas Kiarostami**, Mehdi Rajaian
Cast: Hossein Yarmohammadi, Andre Govalovish
Black and White, 11 minutes

THE EXPERIENCE (1973)
Iran
Production Company: Kanun Parvaresh Fekri
Director: **Abbas Kiarostami**
Screenplay: **Abbas Kiarostami** (based on a story by Amir Naderi)
Cinematography: Ali Reza Zarrindast
Editing: Mehdi Rejaian
Cast: Hassan Yar-Mohamadi, Parvis Naderi, Andrew Guvalovich
Black and White, 60 minutes

THE TRAVELER (1974)
Iran
Production Company: Kanun Parvaresh Fekri
Producer: **Abbas Kiarostami**
Director: **Abbas Kiarostami**
Screenplay: **Abbas Kiarostami** (based on a story by Hassan Rafie)
Cinematography: Fruz Malekzadeh
Editing: Amir Hossein Hami
Music: Kambiz Roshanravan
Cast: Hasan Darabi, Masud Zand Pegleh
Black and White, 83 minutes

SO CAN I (1975)
Iran
Production Company: Kanun Parvaresh Fekri
Director: **Abbas Kiarostami**
Screenplay: **Abbas Kiarostami**
Cinematography: Mostafa Jaji
Editing: **Abbas Kiarostami**
Music: Nasser Cheshmazar
Animation: Farzaneh Taghavi
Cast: Kamal Riahi, Ahmad Kiarostami
Color, 4 minutes

TWO SOLUTIONS FOR ONE PROBLEM (1975)
Iran
Production Company: Kanun Parvaresh Fekri
Director: **Abbas Kiarostami**
Screenplay: **Abbas Kiarostami**
Cinematography: Morteza Rastegar
Editing: **Abbas Kiarostami**
Cast: Sahid and Hamid (full names unavailable)
Color, 5 minutes

A WEDDING SUIT (1976)
Iran
Production Company: Kanun Parvaresh Fekri
Producers: Ebrahim Forouzesh, **Abbas Kiarostami**
Director: **Abbas Kiarostami**
Screenplay: Parviz Davayi, **Abbas Kiarostami**
Cinematography: Foirouz Malekzadeh
Editing: Mousa Afshar, **Abbas Kiarostami**
Cast: Mohammad Fazih Motaleb
Color, 54 minutes

HOW TO MAKE USE OF LEISURE TIME (1977)
Iran
Production Company: Kanun Parvaresh Fekri
Director: **Abbas Kiarostami**
Color, 7 minutes

THE COLORS (1977)
Iran
Production Company: Kanun Parvaresh Fekri
Director: **Abbas Kiarostami**
Screenplay: **Abbas Kiarostami**
Cinematography: Morteza Rastegar, Mostafa Haji
Editing: **Abbas Kiarostami**
Cast: Shahin Amir-Arjomand
Color, 16 minutes

TRIBUTE TO THE TEACHERS (1977)
Iran
Production Company: Kanun Parvaresh Fekri

Director: **Abbas Kiarostami**
Screenplay: **Abbas Kiarostami**
Color, 20 minutes

JAHAN-NAMA PALACE (1977)
Iran
Production Company: Kanun Parvaresh Fekri
Director: **Abbas Kiarostami**
Screenplay: **Abbas Kiarostami**
Color, 30 minutes

THE REPORT (1977)
Iran
Producer: Bahman Farmanara
Director: **Abbas Kiarostami**
Screenplay: **Abbas Kiarostami**
Cinematography: Ali Reza Zarindast
Editing: Mah-Talat Mirfendereski
Cast: Shohreh Aghashlu, Kurosh Afsharpanah
Color, 112 minutes

SOLUTION (1978)
Iran
Production Company: Kanun Parvaresh Fekri
Director: **Abbas Kiarostami**
Screenplay: **Abbas Kiarostami**
Cinematography: Firuz Malekzadeh
Editing: **Abbas Kiarostami**
Color, 11 minutes

CASE #1, CASE #2 / FIRST CASE, SECOND CASE (1979)
Iran
Production Company: Kanun Parvaresh Fekri
Director: **Abbas Kiarostami**
Screenplay: **Abbas Kiarostami**
Cinematography: Houshang Baharalou
Editing: **Abbas Kiarostami**
Cast: Mehdi Azadbakht, Mohammadreza Barati, Hedayat Matin Daftari
Color, 53 minutes

TOOTHACHE (1980)
Iran
Production Company: Kanun Parvaresh Fekri
Director: **Abbas Kiarostami**
Screenplay: **Abbas Kiarostami**
Cinematography: Firuz Malekzadeh
Color, 25 minutes

ORDERLY OR DISORDERLY / REGULARLY OR IRREGULARLY (1981)
Iran
Production Company: Kanun Parvaresh Fekri
Director: **Abbas Kiarostami**
Screenplay: **Abbas Kiarostami**
Color, 17 minutes

THE CHORUS (1982)
Iran
Production Company: Kanun Parvaresh Fekri
Director: **Abbas Kiarostami**
Screenplay: **Abbas Kiarostami** (based on story by Mohammad Javad Kahnemoie)
Cinematography: Ali Reza Zarindast
Editing: **Abbas Kiarostami**
Cast: Yusef Moqaddam
Color, 17 minutes

FELLOW CITIZENS (1983)
Iran
Production Company: Kanun Parvaresh Fekri
Director: **Abbas Kiarostami**
Screenplay: **Abbas Kiarostami**
Cinematography: Firuz Malekzadeh
Cast: Reza Mansuri
Color, 48 minutes

FIRST GRADERS (1984)
Iran
Production Company: Kanun Parvaresh Fekri
Director: **Abbas Kiarostami**
Screenplay: **Abbas Kiarostami**

Cinematography: Homayun Payvar
Editing: **Abbas Kiarostami**
Cast: Tohid School (teachers, staff, and students)
Color, 85 minutes

THE KEY (1987)
Iran
Director: Ebrahim Forouzesh
Screenplay: **Abbas Kiarostami**
Color, 76 minutes

WHERE IS THE FRIEND'S HOUSE? / WHERE IS THE FRIEND'S HOME? (1987)
Iran
Production Companies: Kanun Parvaresh Fekri, Farabi Cinema Foundation
Producer: Ali Reza Zarrin
Director: **Abbas Kiarostami**
Screenplay: **Abbas Kiarostami**
Cinematography: Majod Farzaneh or Farhad Saba
Editing: **Abbas Kiarostami**
Music: Amin Allah Hossein
Cast: Babak Ahmadpour, Ahmad Ahmadpour
Color, 83 minutes

HOMEWORK (1989)
Iran
Production Company: Kanun Parvaresh Fekri
Producer: Ali Reza Zarrin
Director: **Abbas Kiarostami**
Screenplay: **Abbas Kiarostami**
Cinematography: Ali Ashgar Mirza, Iraj Safavi
Editing: **Abbas Kiarostami**, Yava Toorang
Music: Mohammad Reza Aligholi
Color, 86 minutes

CLOSE-UP (1990)
Iran
Production Company: Kanun Parvaresh Fekri
Producer: Ali Reza Zarrin

Director: **Abbas Kiarostami**
Screenplay: **Abbas Kiarostami**
Cinematography: Ali Reza Zarrindast
Editing: **Abbas Kiarostami**
Music: Kambiz Roushanavan
Cast: Hossein Sabzian, Mohsen Makhmalbaf
Color and Black and White, 98 minutes

AND LIFE GOES ON (1992)
Iran
Production Company: Kanun Parvaresh Fekri
Producer: Ali Reza Zarrin
Director: **Abbas Kiarostami**
Screenplay: **Abbas Kiarostami**
Cinematography: Homayoun Pievar
Editing: **Abbas Kiarostami**, Changiz Sayad
Cast: Farhad Kheradmand, Pouya Payvar, Hossein Rezai, and residents of the towns of Koker, Poshteh, Rahmatabad, Rostamabad, and Rudbar
Color, 95 minutes

THE WHITE BALLOON (1995)
Iran, France
Director: Jafar Panahi
Screenplay: Jafar Panahi, **Abbas Kiarostami**
Color, 85 minutes

THROUGH THE OLIVE TREES (1995)
Iran, France
Production Companies: Abbas Kiarostami Productions, CiBy 2000, Farabi Cinema Foundation
Producers: Alain Depardieu, **Abbas Kiarostami**
Director: **Abbas Kiarostami**
Screenplay: **Abbas Kiarostami**
Cinematography: Hossein Jafarian, with Farhad Saba, Bahram Badakhshani, Farzad Jodat
Editing: **Abbas Kiarostami**
Music: Amir Farshid Rahimian, Chema Reosas
Cast: Mohamad Ali Keshavarz, Farhad Kheradmand
Color, 103 minutes

A PROPOS DE NICE, LA SUITE—SEGMENT "REPÉRAGES" (1995)
France
Director: **Abbas Kiarostami**
Color, 100 minutes
(Not listed on the Kiarostami Foundation website)

LUMIÈRE AND COMPANY—SEGMENT "DINNER FOR ONE" (1995)
France, Denmark, Spain, Sweden
Production Companies: Cinétévé, La Sept-Arte, Igeldo Kummunikazio, Søren Stærmose AM, Canal+, ARTE. Eurimages, Musée du Cinéma de Lyon
Producers: Ángel Amigo, Anne Andreu, Humbert Balsan, Neal Edelstein, Fabienne Servan-Schreiber, Søren Stærmose
Directors: **Abbas Kiarostami** and thirty-nine others, including James Ivory and Peter Greenaway
Screenplay: Philippe Pulet
Cinematography: Didier Ferry, Jean-Yves Le Mender, Frédéric MeClair, Sarah Moon, Sven Nykvist, Philippe Pulet
Editing: Roger Ikhlef, Timothy Miller
Music: Jean-Jacques Lemêtre
Color and Black & White, 88 minutes

THE JOURNEY / SAFAR (1996)
Iran
Production Company: Hamrah Filmmaking Group
Director: Alireza Raisian
Screenplay: **Abbas Kiarostami**
Cinematography: Farhad Saba
Editing: Hossein Zandbaf
Music: Kayvan Jahanshahi
Color, 84 minutes

TASTE OF CHERRY (1997)
Iran, France
Production Companies: Abbas Kiarostami Productions, CiBy 2000, Kanun Parvaresh Fekri
Producers: Alain Depardieu, **Abbas Kiarostami**
Director: **Abbas Kiarostami**
Screenplay: **Abbas Kiarostami**
Cinematography: Homayun Payvar
Editing: **Abbas Kiarostami**

Cast: Homayoun Ershadi
Color, 95 minutes

THE BIRTH OF LIGHT (1997)
Iran
Production Company: Waka Film
Director: **Abbas Kiarostami**
Color, 5 minutes

THE WIND WILL CARRY US (1999)
Iran, France
Production Company: mk2
Producers: Marin Karmitz, **Abbas Kiarostami**
Director: **Abbas Kiarostami**
Screenplay: **Abbas Kiarostami** (based on idea by Mahmoud Aiden)
Cinematography: Mahmud Kalari
Editing: **Abbas Kiarostami**
Music: Peyman Yazdanian
Cast: Behzad Dorani
Color, 118 minutes

WILLOW AND WIND (2000)
Iran, Japan
Production Companies: Cima Media International, NHK
Director: Mohammad Ali Talebi
Screenplay: **Abbas Kiarostami**
Cinematography: Farhad Saba
Editing: Sohrab Mirsepassi, Mohammad Ali Talebi
Music: Merhad Jenabi
Cast: Hadi Alipour
Color, 83 minutes

ABC AFRICA (2001)
Iran
Production Companies: IFAD, mk2
Producers: Marin Karmitz, **Abbas Kiarostami**
Director: **Abbas Kiarostami**
Screenplay: **Abbas Kiarostami**
Cinematography: **Abbas Kiarostami**, Seiffollah Samadian
Editing: **Abbas Kiarostami**

Cast: **Abbas Kiarostami**, Seifollah Samadian
Color, 85 minutes

TEN (2002)
Iran, France
Production Companies: Abbas Kiarostami Productions, Key Lime Productions, mk2
Producers: Marin Karmitz, **Abbas Kiarostami**, Nathalie Kreuther, Caley Thomas
Director: **Abbas Kiarostami**
Screenplay: **Abbas Kiarostami**
Cinematography: **Abbas Kiarostami**
Editing: Vahid Ghazi, **Abbas Kiarostami**, Bahman Kiarostami
Music: Howard Blake
Cast: Mania Akbari, Amin Maher
Color, 89 minutes

THE DESERTED STATION (2002)
Iran
Production Companies: Farabi Cinema Foundation, Iranian Independents
Producer: Hossein Zandbaf
Director: Alireza Raisian
Screenplay: Kambuzia Partovi (based on a story by **Abbas Kiarostami**)
Cinematography: Mahammad Aladpoush
Editing: Hossein Zandbaf
Music: Peyman Yazdanian
Cast: Leila Hatami, Nezam Manouchehri
Color, 93 minutes

CRIMSON GOLD (2003)
Iran
Production Company: Jafar Panahi Film Productions
Producer: Jafar Panahi
Director: Jafar Panahi
Screenplay: **Abbas Kiarostami**
Cinematography: Hossein Jafarian
Editing: Jafar Panahi
Music: Peyman Yazdanian
Cast: Hossein Emadeddin
Color, 95 minutes

FIVE DEDICATED TO OZU (2003)
Iran, Japan, France
Production Companies: Behnegar, NHK, mk2
Director: **Abbas Kiarostami**
Screenplay: **Abbas Kiarostami**
Color, 74 minutes

10 ON TEN (2004)
Iran, France
Production Company: mk2
Producer: Marin Karmitz
Director: **Abbas Kiarostami**
Screenplay: **Abbas Kiarostami**
Cast: **Abbas Kiarostami**, Mania Akbari
Color, 88 minutes

TICKETS (2005)
Italy, UK
Production Companies: Fandango, Medusa Film, Sixteen Films
Producer: Carlo Cresto-Dina, Babak Karimi, Rebecca O'Brien, Domenico Procacci, Paul Trijbits
Directors: **Abbas Kiarostami**, Ken Loach, Ermanno Olmi
Screenplay: Ermanno Olmi, **Abbas Kiarostami**, Paul Laverty
Cinematography: Mahmoud Kalari, Chris Menges, Fabio Olmi
Editing: Babak Karimi, Jonathan Morris, Giovanni Ziberna
Music: George Fenton
Cast: Carlo Delle Piane, Valeria Bruni Tedeschi
Color, 109 minutes

MEN AT WORK (2006)
Iran
Production Companies: Aftab Negaran Institute, Aftab Negaran Productions
Producer: Mohammad Reza Takhtkeshian
Director: Mani Haghighi
Screenplay: Mani Haghighi, **Abbas Kiarostami**
Cinematography: Kooyar Kalari
Editing: Mastaneh Mahajer
Cast: **Abbas Kiarostami**
Color, 75 minutes

ROADS OF KIAROSTAMI (2006)
Iran
Production Company: Abbas Kiarostami Productions
Director: **Abbas Kiarostami**
Screenplay: **Abbas Kiarostami**
Cinematography: **Abbas Kiarostami**
Editing: **Abbas Kiarostami**
Cast: **Abbas Kiarostami** (uncredited)
Color and Black and White, 32 minutes

ERICE—KIAROSTAMI: CORRESPONDENCES (2006)
Iran, Spain
Production Company: CCCB
Directors: **Abbas Kiarostami**, Víctor Erice
Screenplay: **Abbas Kiarostami**, Víctor Erice
Cinematography: **Abbas Kiarostami**, Víctor Erice
Editing: **Abbas Kiarostami**, Víctor Erice
Color, 97 minutes

PERSIAN CARPET (2007)—segment "Is There a Place to Approach?"
Iran
Production Companies: National Iranian Carpet Center, Farabi Cinema Foundation
Producer: Reza Mirkarimi
Directors: **Abbas Kiarostami** and twelve others
Screenplay: **Abbas Kiarostami**
Cinematography: Sarsan Tavakkoli Farsi
Music: Perviz Yahaghi
Color, 117 minutes (6 min segment)

TO EACH HIS OWN CINEMA (2007)—segment "Where Is My Romeo?"
France
Production Companies: Cannes Film Festival, Elzévir Films
Producer: Jacques Arhex
Directors: **Abbas Kiarostami** and thirty-two others
Music: Mark Bradshaw, Mychael Danna, Eleni Karaindrou, Howard Shore
Color and Black and White, 100 minutes
(Not listed on the Kiarostami Foundation website)

SHIRIN (2008)
Iran
Production Company: Abbas Kiarostami Productions
Producers: **Abbas Kiarostami**, Hamideh Razavi
Director: **Abbas Kiarostami**
Screenplay: **Abbas Kiarostami**, Farideh Golbou
Cinematography: Hoohman Mehmanesh, Mahmoud Kalari
Editing: **Abbas Kiarostami**, Arash Sadeghi
Color, 92 minutes

CERTIFIED COPY (2010)
France, Italy, Belgium, Iran
Production Companies: mk2, BiBi Film, France 3 Cinéma, Artémis Productions
Producers: Angelo Barbagello, Charles Gillibert, Marin Karmitz, **Abbas Kiarostami**, Nathanaël Karmitz
Director: **Abbas Kiarostami**
Screenplay: **Abbas Kiarostami**, Caroline Eliacheff
Cinematography: Luca Bigazzi
Editing: Bahman Kiarostami
Cast: Juliette Binoche, William Shimell
Color, 106 minutes

NO (2010)
France
Production Company: Zadig Productions
Producer: Mélanie Gerin
Director: **Abbas Kiarostami**
Color, 8 minutes

MEETING LEILA (2012)
Iran
Production Company: Honar va Tajrobe
Producer: Adel Yaraghi
Director: Adel Yaraghi
Screenplay: **Abbas Kiarostami**, Adel Yaraghi
Cinematography: Alireza Barazandeh, Reza Teimouri
Editing: Parham Vafaee, Adel Yaraghi
Cast: Meila Hatami, Adel Yaraghi
Color, 87 minutes

LIKE SOMEONE IN LOVE (2012)
Japan, France
Production Companies: Centre National du Cinéma et de l'Image Animée, Euro Space, mk2 Productions
Producers: Marin Karmitz, **Abbas Kiarostami**
Directors: **Abbas Kiarostami**, Banafsheh Violet
Screenplay: **Abbas Kiarostami**, Mohammad Rahmani
Cinematography: Katsumi Yanagijima
Editing: Bahman Kiarostami
Cast: Tadashi Okuno, Rin Takanashi
Color, 109 minutes

VENICE 70: FUTURE RELOADED (2013)—one segment
Italy, USA, Ethiopia, Samoa, UK, Iran, China, Israel, Austria, Russia, Germany, Algeria, Thailand, Japan, Belgium, Greece, India, Spain, Hong Kong
Production Companies: Avventurosa, Dream Film, IbiscusMedia, Watchmen Productions
Directors: **Abbas Kiarostami** and sixty-nine others
Screenplay: **Abbas Kiarostami**
Cast: Shahed Sherafat, Amir Hoseein Mohammad Nejad, Mani Sherafat
Color, 120 minutes (85-sec segment)

SEAGULL EGGS (2014)
Iran
Production Company: Abbas Kiarostami Productions
Director: **Abbas Kiarostami**
Screenplay: **Abbas Kiarostami**
Color, 17 minutes
(Not listed on the Kiarostami Foundation website)

PASAJERA (2016)
Cuba
Production Company: Abbas Kiarostami Productions
Director: **Abbas Kiarostami**
Color, 97 minutes
(Only listed on the Kiarostami Foundation website)

TAKE ME HOME (2016)
Iran
Production Company: Abbas Kiarostami Productions
Director: **Abbas Kiarostami**
Black and White, 16 minutes

24 FRAMES (2017)
Iran, France
Production Companies: Kiarostami Foundation, CG Cinéma, Eggplant Picture & Sound
Producers: Charles Gillibert, Ahmad Kiarostami
Director: **Abbas Kiarostami**
Cinematography: Dariush Gorji Zadeh, Peyman Solhi, Delaram Delashob, Yousef Khoshnaghsh
Cast: Farhad Farhadi, Salma Mansh, Shabnam Bazigar
Color and Black and White, 114 minutes

Abbas Kiarostami: Interviews

The Camera of Art—An Interview with Abbas Kiarostami

Miriam Rosen / 1991

From *Cineaste*, vol. 19, no. 2/3, 25th Anniversary Issue (1992), pp. 38–40. Reprinted by permission.

As Abbas Kiarostami notes, with an evident mix of surprise and satisfaction, Iran's major exports now include pistachio nuts, carpets, oil . . . and films. Although film production came to a virtual standstill after the Revolution of 1978–79, and the new government's earliest attempts to create a cinema in its own image met with little success among local audiences and foreign festivals alike, films of quality began to (re)appear relatively soon. With Amir Naderi's *The Runner* (*Devandeh*, 1985), shown at the Venice, London and Nantes film festivals, and the nearly two dozen films that followed in the international festival circuit over the next five years, the outlines of a "new" Iranian cinema began to be perceived abroad. To be sure, a talented younger generation has emerged since the Revolution, most notably with Mohsen Makhmalbaf, whose *The Peddler* (*Dastforush*, 1986) and *Marriage of the Blessed* (*Arusi-ye khuban*, 1989) traveled through the US with the "Recent Iranian Cinema" series in 1990–91, or the two women directors included in the same series, Rakhshan Banietemad (*Off the Limits* [*Kharej az madudeh*, 1989]) and Puran Darakhshandeh (*Lost Time* [*Zaman-e az dast rafteh*, 1989]). But if the Islamic Republic has taken exemplary initiatives in the production and promotion of films (with all of the control and self-promotion that these imply), the cinema itself is rather strikingly continuous with the finest achievements of the pre-Revolutionary era, and many of the most prominent directors have long careers behind them.

A distinguished case in point is provided by Abbas Kiarostami, whose most recent films, the fictional *Where Is the Friend's Home?* (*Khaneh-ye dust kojast?*, 1986), the documentary *Homework* (*Mashq-e shah*, 1990), and the unclassifiable *Close-Up* (*Nema-ye nazdik*, 1990), have cumulatively catapulted the director into the forefront of the international art film circuit. At this year's Cannes

Film Festival, the director was awarded the prestigious Rossellini Prize. In fact, Kiarostami has been working for the last twenty-two years at the Institute for the Intellectual Development of Children and Young Adults, and, during this time, he has made some fourteen shorts and medium-length films and six features, including the newly completed *And Life Goes On* (*Zendegi va digar hich*, 1992).

Born in Tehran in 1940, he trained in graphic arts and divided his time between poster design, children's book illustration, and advertising films until he was invited to set up a film unit at the Institute for the Intellectual Development of Children and Young Adults in 1969. As he indicates, nearly all of his films originate in his immediate experience, from (cleverly) educational shorts—*Dental Hygiene* (*Behdasht-e dandan*, 1980), for example, was inspired by his young son's request to be excused from brushing his teeth one night—to features like *Where Is the Friend's Home?*, which combines an incident involving his son and a school teacher's short story within the allegorical structure of a mystical tale.

Given that his actors are always nonprofessionals and most often children, the dividing line between fiction and documentary is never very clear, and Kiarostami himself refuses to make the distinction. At the very playful beginning of *Homework*—which gradually turns into a terrifying indictment of the educational system—Kiarostami and his crew make their way to the elementary school where the film is to be shot, and, in response to a curious passerby, the director explains, in voice-over, that he's interested in the issue of homework because of problems he'd had with his own son, but he doesn't know yet whether with fiction or documentary. And with *Close-Up* (Grand Prize winner at Montreal in 1990, also shown last year at Filmfest, DC), he finally managed to do both. The point of departure for this film was in fact a stranger-than-fiction news item about an unemployed printer who had unsuccessfully attempted to pass himself off as film director Mohsen Makhmalbaf. As Kiarostami tells the story, he was about to start shooting another film when he literally told the producer that he'd changed his mind and took the crew to the prison where the unlucky imposter, Hossein Sabzian, was awaiting trial. After this initial encounter, recorded with a hidden camera, he convinced the judge to let him film the trial (which turned into a ten hour shooting session), and subsequently got all of his protagonists to reenact the events leading up to what he had actually been able to film. The resulting "close-up" is in fact a mirror, not only of the principals involved, but also of the larger society, of the director himself, and of contemporary cinema in Iran.

Abbas Kiarostami spoke with Miriam Rosen in Paris in October 1991, on the occasion of the seventh annual Iranian Film Festival held at the Utopia Champollion cinema. Translation from the Persian, along with a great deal of background information, was provided by the festival's organizer, Mamad Haghighat.

Cineaste: What does the title *Close-Up* mean to you?

Abbas Kiarostami: It has to do with the fact that in my regular life, outside of filmmaking, I don't like people to be far away, like in a long shot. When I see these same people, people I know, much closer, my feelings about them change. I think that when people are in a close-up, it's different from when you see them in a long shot, and you can understand them better. So a close-up means coming as close as possible to someone. If you look at the Sabzian affair from a distance, for example, you'd say that he's a crook, a charlatan, and so forth. But when you come nearer to him, when you have a close-up of him, you see that it isn't true. That's why I called the film *Close-Up*.

Cineaste: But in that sense you could have given the same title to all of your films, couldn't you?

Kiarostami: But this time, in *Close-Up*, there was a preexisting attitude, a particular prejudice, when the affair was seen from a distance, and so the idea of the close-up corresponded much better to this film. I used a separate camera, the one that you actually see in the front of the courtroom, so that Sabzian could explain everything he wanted to say. What other people might not believe, at least he could say it to that camera.

Cineaste: But isn't there a metaphorical level, too? The film is also a close-up of the society, and this closeness to reality, the engagement with what actually exists, seems characteristic of Iranian films today.

Kiarostami: That's right. This is the level that usually makes art. The other camera is the camera of judgment, but I'm not concerned with the fact that the people who made the law are rather cruel. This is the camera of art, and it comes much closer to people and lets them explain things that they couldn't explain to the judge or the jury. So here the camera as close-up lets people talk about their real problems. That's what's important. The best thing that art can do is to give people detailed knowledge, not to make judgments. This knowledge might be about myself, or about my son, for example, or about the life of a couple; these are things that wouldn't ordinarily be known, but the camera lets them circulate among other human beings. This is an important role for art.

Cineaste: You've talked about Iran's millennial culture as a backdrop for the contemporary cinema. Can you explain how the cinema draws on the various elements of that culture, whether literature or art or daily life?

Kiarostami: It's a whole; you can't break it down into such-and-such a percentage. For me, the two most important elements come from looking at daily life and looking within myself. I can see myself in all the characters in *Close-Up*: for example, I see myself lying, and, at the same time, I see myself being lied to by other people. Sometimes I do the same thing as Sabzian—when I'm unhappy; with myself, I'd like to be someone else. I've even copied someone else's poems and said that I'm the one who wrote them. So there's a part of each one of these characters in me. That's why I know them so well.

Cineaste: Have you always edited your films yourself?

Kiarostami: Always.

Cineaste: What does editing mean for you in the creation of a film? It seems very particular in the ones I've seen.

Kiarostami: Basically, editing means eliminating certain things and bringing others together. It's the same thing in my films. But since I have a certain difficulty communicating with another person, I'd rather do the editing myself, until I manage to find someone that I have a good understanding with. Besides, I don't have a precise script that an editor can use for the shooting script. I shoot quickly, and I don't have a lot of time to prepare what I want to do, so sometimes that creates certain problems when I start editing. But that difficulty is just for me; I'm the one who knows exactly what I have to do with the materials I have.

Cineaste: There was a break in film production after the Iranian Revolution, but as time goes on, it seems that there's not really a break in Iranian cinema. What do you think?

Kiarostami: The Revolution, this Islamic period, hasn't had the same influence on everyone. People who didn't have that much originality in their work are doing things differently today—they change their subjects or their techniques. But for people like myself, it's the continuation of the same line. If you could see the films I made before, that would confirm the unity, the harmony, in my work. It's pretty much the same for the known filmmakers—Amir Naderi, for example, is someone who's followed the same path, who's always maintained his spirit, his harmony.

Cineaste: I have the impression that the preoccupations are the same, too.

Kiarostami: In my opinion, the real filmmakers still have the same concerns, before and after. It's personal work, this business of filmmaking. If they take it seriously, then they're going to do the same thing before or after. But the ones who didn't have their own approach, their own concerns, well, they've changed.

Cineaste: The constraints aren't exactly new, either, are they? There was already censorship under the Shah, but it seems to me that there's a whole tradition in Iranian culture, a style of speaking indirectly.

Kiarostami: I have two things to say about that kind of symbolic style. On the one hand, there are symbols that are rather weak, and not very interesting. Sometimes people find symbolic aspects in my films that I don't agree with. They come from the minds of the people looking at the film, their way of interpreting. Nonetheless, in systems where there is a kind of repression, you always have to make a detour to explain what you want, to pass through signs, symbols, metaphors, all of that. Sometimes filmmakers use certain symbols thinking that the public will understand and the government won't, but the government is part of the public, too, and they're going to understand. In general, I don't agree with symbolic or metaphoric cinema used in a conscious way. Personally, that kind of expression only gets interesting for me when it comes from my unconscious. Sometimes people tell me things about my film that, when I look at it again, I see that, yes, they're right, and I realize that it came from my unconscious.

Cineaste: The metaphor or the symbol is just one way of saying things without saying them. There's also simply what isn't said, which comes back to the question of editing—you take things out, and the public learns to put them back in.

Kiarostami: There are two issues here: the complexity of certain works of art shouldn't be confused with symbolism. That complexity is part of the essence of art, and I can't talk about it. That's what allows the viewers to interpret what they want, with their own vision. It's possible that the creator, the artist, didn't intend to say that, but it can also come from the unconscious. Let's take an example in *Close-Up*. In Iran, one scene was interpreted very strangely—when there's a little bottle that rolls down the street. People gave that a very important, very political significance, but that wasn't at all my intention. A lot of people asked me what it means, and I said, "Nothing, it doesn't mean anything." So people said, "Then why did you put that scene there?" And my answer is that there can also be a scene that doesn't mean anything because, in this case, for example, inside the house, something very important was happening—Sabzian was being arrested—and the viewers would naturally want to see what was going on inside. I wanted to show something else at the same time, precisely so that the viewer would ask what's going on inside. There was a sloping street, and a little bottle that could roll down to the end, and I just wanted to play with it a little. But in Iran, everyone has a completely different interpretation. They're free to think what they want. The danger comes when someone wants to say, "No, my interpretation is the only right one."

Cineaste: Sometimes I have the impression that Iranian cinema is strong not in spite of the constraints, but because of them.

Kiarostami: When you don't have any limits, when you're not a little blocked, sometimes you can't work either. If I have a subject that doesn't come up against censorship, I feel like I haven't thought it through enough. But when you really think, when you really reflect on what you want to do, sometimes you go right past the censors. They can stop the most primitive and superficial things, but, if you really reflect, you can always get past this stage of censorship. That's what makes art stronger. Some people believe that a work of art—a committed film, for example—should overthrow a regime. In my opinion, a committed film just provides certain knowledge about human beings and their environment, that's all. We've seen that the Revolution hasn't been able to solve the problems. What each one of us can do is to try to improve ourselves, to go forward. You have to start with yourself. That's how I see a committed work of art.

Cineaste: What about the restrictions on the representation of women? This is one very tangible change since the Revolution. Do you think it presents a real obstacle for a filmmaker?

Kiarostami: Yes and no. Yes, there's a problem with filming women in Iran. Sometimes it happens that I can't make the films I want; if a project is directly about a young woman, for example, I put it aside. But that doesn't keep me from working as a filmmaker. This is not the essential problem for us. In Iranian society, there are so many problems, thousands and thousands, and that's one of them, but if the others get resolved, the problem of the Islamic veil will also get resolved automatically. It might take five hundred years; it's necessary to wait.

There's a woman I know who had her breasts removed because of cancer, and when she heard other women talking about the Islamic veil, she said, "I don't understand what you're saying. I don't have a problem with the Islamic veil, because I have a much bigger problem." Sometimes a social problem is as serious as cancer. In *Homework*, for example, if you pay attention to the education of children, for a country which has the youngest population in the world, the Islamic veil is less important than education for so many young people.

Cineaste: There also seems to be a dramatic change—a positive one—in the level of film culture in Iran. Where do you think this new public has come from?

Kiarostami: For one thing, after the Revolution, the religious ban on families going to the cinema was lifted, and that created a new public.[1] Now there's an extraordinary thirst for culture and for the cinema in Iran. Even we filmmakers are surprised. Sometimes films like those of Tarkovsky or Bergman play for a very long time, and there are many books published about them. People read, they reread, they see the films again—it's astonishing, this thirst for cinema today. Perhaps it also comes from the fact that there's political repression in Iran, and people are demoralized about other things, so they take refuge in the movie theatres. Personally, I think that art and politics are complementary: when one of them doesn't function any more, the other one takes over and attracts more people. Don't forget, too, that the cinema in Iran is the least expensive form of entertainment.

Cineaste: But the phenomenon isn't just quantitative; it's also qualitative. In *Close-Up*, for example, the whole episode revolves around the fact that a filmmaker is so highly esteemed that he's worth impersonating. How do you explain this situation?

Kiarostami: If we were talking about art or literature, I could tell you that we have a historical background. But for film, we're astonished too. Iranian cinema has been making its way all over the world for a while now. I think of it as one of Iran's major exports: in addition to pistachio nuts, carpets, and oil, now there's the cinema. It's important, and encouraging, but I can't tell you where it comes from. Someone on the outside might be able to explain, but those of us on the inside are just amazed, and very pleased about it.

Note

1. Historically condemned by members of Iran's religious establishment, the cinema was in effect rehabilitated by Ayatollah Khomeini after the Revolution: "We are not opposed to cinema, to radio, or to television," he declared in his very first speech after his return to Iran. "The cinema is a modern invention that ought to be used for the sake of educating the people.... It is the misuse of cinema that we are opposed to." Following this pronouncement, and widely circulated reports of his enthusiasm for Dariush Mehrjui's classic *The Cow* (*Gav*, 1969), religious families that had never watched films before began going regularly to the cinema. Khomeini's speech is cited by Hamid Naficy in the program notes for the L.A. film series, reprinted in *Jusur: The UCLA Journal of Middle Eastern Studies* (no. 6, 1990).

Abbas Kiarostami by Akram Zaatari

BOMB / 1995

This interview was commissioned by and first published in BOMB, no. 50, Winter 1995. © BOMB Magazine, New Art Publications, and its contributors. All rights reserved. The BOMB Digital Archive can be viewed at www.bombmagazine.org.

With minimal dialogue, non-professional actors, and practically no written script, Abbas Kiarostami plots an innocent world where modest characters live complex, layered lives. While Kiarostami mixes documentary and fiction fluently, he admits his failure in revealing the "truth" through cinema. But this search takes him from one film to another. Born and based in Teheran, Iran, Kiarostami started making films in the early 1970s, when he founded the film department of the Centre of Intellectual Development of Children and Young Adults. While his work transcends the specificity of locale, his latest film, *Through the Olive Trees*, is the result of an emotional attachment to Koker, the rural part of Iran where he shot two of his earlier films, *Where Is the Friend's House?* (1987) and *Life Goes On* (1989) [this film is now distributed under the title *And Life Goes On*]. An intricate puzzle of narratives unfolding with one another, each film reveals what was faked in the previous one, but also fabricates a new lie. *Life Goes On* revisits the area of *Friend's House*, and shows that its characters have their own life outside the film they are creating. *Through the Olive Trees* is, in turn, about how *Life Goes On* was made. In *Olive Trees*, Kiarostami shows a scene being shot from *Life Goes On* in which Hossein and Tahareh, who play a married couple, argue off camera. After the scene has been shot, Hossein returns to his role as the film's production assistant and makes tea for the crew. A continuous shot follows his tea tray around the set and then finally up a staircase where he places a flower next to the last glass of tea for Tahareh. She responds with negative silence. As often happens in the cinema of Abbas Kiarostami, the real drama was taking place after the cameras stopped rolling. Or was it?

Akram Zaatari: I would like to know more about your idea of the film and the lie. Let's start with *Close-Up* in which a man fabricates a lie out of his passion for cinema and hence makes his own film. One of the powerful points of *Close-Up* for me was the fact that it merges film and life. *Through the Olive Trees*, on the other hand, presents itself clearly as the making of a film. What's different in the second approach?

Abbas Kiarostami: Our work starts with a lie on a daily routine basis. When you make a film you bring elements from other places, other environments, and you gather them together in a unity that really doesn't exist. You're faking that unity. You call someone a husband or a son.

My own son was critical of me because in the second film, *Life Goes On*, I hint that these two people are married, and that's what I lead the audience to believe at the end of that film. In *Through the Olive Trees*, I come up with the idea that they are not really married, and it's just the boy who is really fascinated by the girl. In my next film, I'm going to show another layer of truth in that actually the boy is not really that crazy about the girl. So, my son is critical that I keep lying to people, that I keep changing. In the next film it's really the girl who loves the boy. My son concluded that perhaps if we analyze different aspects of the lie, then we can arrive at the truth. In cinema anything that can happen would be true. It doesn't have to correspond to a reality, it doesn't have to "really" be happening. In cinema, by fabricating lies we may never reach the fundamental truth, but we will always be on our way to it. We can never get close to the truth except through lying.

AZ: You're now working on a fourth addition to what was to be a trilogy. The idea of a film that develops into another film can go on indefinitely. Where are you reaching with this? Is it merely a motivation to make another film?

AK: As long as this series is fresh and has energy, I'll go with it until I'm exhausted. I have had other scripts I have made a commitment to making, but when I finish a film, I still have emotional attachments to elements of that film. So it becomes an edge on my part, to go back to the same story and make another film so I can get it out of my system. When I made the first movie in that trilogy, *Where Is the Friend's House?*, I never felt the certainty and intimacy that I feel now about that particular environment. Back then it presented a new environment, new people, fresh subject matter, but it didn't have the same energy. Now I feel I am much more deeply involved with the actors of this film.

AZ: How did you connect to the narrative of *Through the Olive Trees*?

AK: There was a four-minute scene in *Life Goes On* in which the main character, Hossein, is attracted to Tahereh, the same girl in *Through the Olive Trees*. It was interesting to me that the girl wasn't reacting to him because I was under the impression that in a village community there would be more equality in terms of relationships. You wouldn't see the kind of choices people make in urban environments. But she says, "You're not good enough for me." It was interesting that something like that existed in a village environment.

AZ: How did the narrative evolve from that point? I read that you started with a fifteen-page treatment. What changed between the treatment and the film?

AK: I really wanted to avoid having a film-within-the-film structure but I just couldn't come up with anything else. So, I followed the fifteen-page treatment I had put together, and that was the basis of the film. I wrote those fifteen pages as an encouragement to the cast and crew so they could base their work on something. But as far as I'm concerned, I'd be fine with only five pages of material. That provides enough of a narrative foundation. If you write something well in advance, you develop a fixation and a sense of commitment to it that might restrict your freedom in terms of improvising or coming up with new ideas. I like to save that kind of freedom for when I shoot the film. When you write a script and think it should be turned into a film word by word, then what is the motivation to go out and turn it into a film?

AZ: You've said that you wrote the dialogue of *Olive Trees*, but in fact it belongs to the non-actors and actors in your film. Can you elaborate on that?

AK: I give them the general subject matter the night before. And I start communicating with them so they can really clear out their minds from any previous exposure to a script. This way they come to the set with a fresh mind. The following day, rehearsing before the shoot, I work on it with them from an entirely different angle. Then, the moment before starting to shoot, I play this trick on them. I say, "Forget about what we just discussed, let's go back to what we discussed last night." The advantage of this technique is that the actors are unable to use memorized words. They know what the idea is, but they have to make up new ways of putting a sentence together. And doing that, they have the same anxieties you would have. So, I simply remind them of a general subject while we're shooting. It's like a computer: you want them to be blank-minded so you program them, then get immediate feedback.

AZ: Both Hossein in *Through the Olive Trees* and Sabzian in *Close-Up* are men who are unsuccessful in their lives. Hossein would like to marry Tahereh, but she refuses him because he doesn't own a house. Sabzian has lost his job and his wife. However, they are both able to realize their dreams through faking reality: Hossein plays the husband of Tahereh in the film shown being made in *Olive Trees*. Sabzian fabricates a lie and lives for a while the way he would like to live, as a director. Your male characters are very modest, except for the filmmaker characters, who operate on a different level and seem able to solve everyone's problems. I would like to know more about the role you attribute to the filmmaker in society.

AK: I can see why you might have misunderstood me in terms of the power I give to the director. In both films, the directors are really the background characters. The real figures come to exist within that background. So the background is just a vehicle. I use the director characters to bring the other characters to the forefront. A director character needs to show some strength and power, some control of the environment. It's only natural that they would be perceived as stronger characters.

AZ: In *Olive Trees*, there are three strong women characters: Tahereh, who refuses to marry Hossein; her stubborn grandmother; and Mrs. Shiva, the assistant director. But these characters, like women characters in your other films, remain opaque and unexplored. Is this deliberate?

AK: Traditionally, in Iranian films, the female characters are portrayed in two categories: as mothers or as mistresses. And in neither of these categories are characters I'd like to use. They lack human dimension. Many Western films suffer from the same shortcomings. Women are treated like cosmetic characters, just to boost box office sales. There are two other types of women characters in Iranian films. The first is the heroic type, which I can't relate to because they're too shrewd. The second is the victim, which again is a type I can't relate to. Outside of these four categories there isn't much left to deal with.

There are exceptional women characters, but then I don't make movies about exceptions. I would like to deal with normal women, and I don't find too many of them. I would like to have that kind of woman character whose womanhood is not an issue, but I just can't find them. There's an Italian actor, Lando Bozanco, whose films are very popular in Iran. His characters are macho and naive at the same time. In Iranian films you have a lot of women who are like that male character. They are too concerned or too much aware of their womanhood, and are somewhat pretentious about it.

AZ: And your male characters are the opposite of that.

AK: They are just normal human beings. Their sexuality is not a question.

AZ: You rely on your own experiences in your films, things that happen within the family or that you observe in society. What do you think outsiders to your culture wouldn't understand in your films?

AK: I normally go with the most commonplace experiences, so every type of audience can relate to them. Can you pinpoint something in particular that you think relates to me personally and would not be visible to other audiences?

AZ: Is there any kind of humor, for example, that specific audiences would or would not react to?

AK: The audiences have different expectations, and it wouldn't be correct to categorize them by the regions they come from. There is a relationship with which I can't interfere between the film and its audience. The movies and the way audiences react to them have to do with the audience's minds, and it's not something we can measure like somebody's shoe size.

AZ: Since you have worked so much with local communities in Iran, do you think you can work in some other society where you haven't lived? Do you think you can come up with plots with the same power?

AK: What is Iranian about *Through the Olive Trees* and *Close-Up*? In *Olive Trees*, there is nothing terribly Iranian about the relationship between Hossein and Tahereh. The same is true about Sabzian and the way he relates to the family. It's not really Iranian. I make my films about human beings and their universality. In that sense I don't restrict myself to a certain area. We may be different in terms of the color of our skins, but we get the same toothaches.

AZ: I think what speaks to the fact that your films do come from a very specific place is the way you examine the tension between tradition and modernity, between rurality and urbanity. The audience is made aware of the presence of new settlements next to a highway. We hear the noise of cars but never see them.

AK: I'm only posing questions by showing those types of conflicts. I would never think of myself as someone who also comes up with some way of resolving them. In a scene in *Olive Trees*, a bunch of girls are dressed in black and later another bunch of children are dressed in bright colors. Compared to the earlier scene in the film where women are dressed in black, I treated the colorful scene with a lot more freedom to evoke an open environment. To me, that is the visual comment I'm making. I react with sorrow to any sort of change that would not be consistent with the freedom of people. When they chop down trees to construct buildings, I feel the same sadness.

AZ: But isn't that the way things have been going for a long time?

AK: That's why I mentioned earlier not to expect a solution or a judgement from me. I feel the same way about the idea of my grandmother's death. I'm really sad, but there is nothing I can do about it. I don't have the power to say, "No, I want to keep her forever." But when she goes, there's no way I would not be sad about it.

AZ: Koker, the area you filmed, was depopulated by the earthquake. I see that as a big problem, but you seem to portray a very embellished image of the post-quake period in Koker. You called that film *Life Goes On*, as if the problems of the earthquake had been overcome, which is not the case.

AK: I would agree with you that I do embellish. Life is alive and well and keeps on going. Life is stronger than death because life is still there. After I made the second film, somebody asked, "When do you think the normal life of these people will resume again?" And I said, "On the third day, when I saw them washing their carpets." But I was mistaken when I talked further with the people. I realized they had stories going back to the time of the earthquake. There was a man who had fallen under a huge piece of metal, and the minute he started to get out from under it to save himself—as far as he's concerned—that's when life started again.

AZ: In the beginning of this interview you mentioned something about your process of filmmaking being very open to change. From casting to editing, a film might transform into a different film. Can you comment more on what qualities this adds to the film? Could it be a film that is more open to interpretation, for example?

AK: I wouldn't know about people's interpretations, but I find it extremely useful in terms of the way I work. It allows me to make those changes. During the film you have Hossein correct the director. He tells him that the girl doesn't have to say "Mr. Hossein" when she addresses him, that "Hossein" is enough. When you don't have a prepared script and are allowing that kind of freedom you can have situations like that. Sometimes we go from Tehran to remote villages, and it would be a mistake for us to go there with preconceptions and the inability to change.

AZ: I wanted to compliment you on the use of sound in your film. Relying on ambient sounds, you rarely use music as an emotional guide.

AK: For some directors the significance of sound is more important than the visual. When we go out to shoot, sometimes people ask the crew where they're going and they say, "We're just going to record some sound, but we're taking a cinematographer with us, just in case." If you just concentrate on the visual, you would be dealing with only one side of the cube. Sometimes we put so much emphasis on our shot, it's as if we're telling the world, "Shut up, the picture is so important!" But if you look at you and me sitting here talking, there are all these noises around us. That's an important part of reality.

Abbas Kiarostami Interview

UNESCO Courier / 1995

From *UNESCO Courier*, July–August 1995, pp. 38–40. Reprinted by permission of *UNESCO Courier*.

UNESCO Courier: Why do you make films?

Abbas Kiarostami: Because I can't do anything else! Making films is something I have to do. It's like dreaming: it comes naturally, it fulfils a need. The driver of an Underground train who spends hours travelling through the dark tunnels dreams all the time. While they're in prison, convicts dream of the world outside. Blind people see by means of dreams. Life is impossible without dreams, and thanks to the cinema I can give shape to some of mine and let others share them. A link with other people is made through my dreams. It's a strange kind of pleasure, communicating with people I don't know and can't see but who can see my dreams....

All artists yearn to communicate. It makes them ill if they can't share their dreams. I must be one of these people. This need links me to my audiences and, first and foremost, to my actors. During filming, and because of it, I empathize so strongly with the actors that they become part of me.

The relationship becomes so intense that when shooting is over I find it impossible to part company with them. That's why my film *Where Is the Friend's Home?* (1987) had two sequels, *And Life Goes On* (1992) and *Under the Olive Trees* (1994) [also known as *Through the Olive Trees*], and will be continued in my future films. I am so fond of the region where these three films were made and the people who live there that I am in no hurry to move on.

What happens behind the camera gives me just as much pleasure as what happens in front of it. Behind it, one catches life unawares; in front, everything is planned and organized, even the actors' feelings and movements. Everything is subordinated to technical requirements. The equipment, the constraints of photography, the overpowering presence of the crew and especially of the director, all affect the actors' attitudes. The liveliness and excitement that are to be found behind the camera often dry up, fade away and die in front of it. We should have to get rid of the film crew and all their paraphernalia before the actors' performance could be the real thing, a true reflection of their identity. Only then could their complex inner life become visible.

People do not know themselves until they get to know their own repressed desires. They have to be revealed to themselves. Before any transformation can take place, we have to know our own legitimate needs, which originate in dreams. Our dreams grow out of the bitter experience of daily life, which they endeavor to transcend by seeking a life of their own.

The cinema can provide a window looking out from the mediocrity of life on to the world of dreams. Reality is the launching pad for dreams. Everything must start from reality, just as you launch a kite into the wind but hold on to the strings. The kite-strings lead us to reality. We enter the dream world and come back to real life.

After dreaming, reality may seem easier to bear, since the change of scene has brought an influx of energy and alleviated the sufferings of everyday existence. On the other hand, reality may seem intolerable, uglier and more oppressive than before—a dead end. If this is the case, then we must change reality. We follow our dream until reality is transformed into dream and dream into reality.

UC: What difficulties are Iranian filmmakers facing today?

AK: First of all, the same difficulties as those faced by filmmakers the world over. No director can be sure his or her film will be a success. Generally speaking, producers want to back a good film, a quality film, but above all a money-spinner—and there's never any guarantee of that. One of the hardest things is to win a producer's confidence.

The difficulties specific to Iran, an Islamic country, are the limits imposed by religion. We filmmakers are great liars; we create lies to suggest truths. We bring in a man from one place and a woman from another, and select a particular house and a particular child to present a true picture of a family. But if the woman has to get out of bed wearing a veil, I am the first to find the scene implausible. I live in an Islamic society and my family are Muslims, but neither my sister nor my wife wear headscarves in bed. So far I have managed to avoid this kind of scene which gives a false picture of reality, but because of these restrictions many subjects are automatically ruled out.

UC: Is that one of the reasons why you work with children?

AK: Not at all. I like working with children. It started quite by chance and then I came to like having them around. They are at ease in front of the camera. They are not thinking about fame or money. They are amenable.

UC: No American films are allowed to be distributed in Iran. What do you think of this ban?

AK: It's both a good thing and a bad thing: good for Iranian filmmakers, who are protected from competition from American films and have been able to make films and win the appreciation of cinema-goers; bad for Iranian audiences, who can never see American pictures at the cinema. The situation clearly has both negative and positive aspects, negative because any ban is undesirable but positive as regards the protection of the Iranian film industry.

UC: Doesn't the fact that people regularly watch foreign films on video stop them going to the cinema?

AK: There is a certain class of people who no longer go to the cinema, who are video consumers. The cassettes are of poor quality. They are recorded abroad direct from television sets and distributed in Iran.

The recent introduction of satellite television has created a flagrant contradiction between what people, young people in particular, see at home and what they see outside the home. To take one example, children are not allowed to go to school in jeans but at home my son can see, on satellite television, images of freedom that constantly conflict with life in Iran. This contradiction is psychologically harmful and wounding for him. It is sad for a filmmaker like me to end up saying that it would be better if we didn't have satellite dishes in Iran. When a balance cannot be struck between the inside and outside, you have to do as best you can, so my son and I agreed that we should shut the television set away in a locked cupboard. But I know that my heart is locked in that cupboard too. While I was out, he opened the cupboard and plugged the set back in.

UC: Who goes to the cinema in Iran?

AK: Ordinary people, the man in the street, the people from the bazaars—what we call the "third class"—but also middle-class people. A film currently showing in Tehran, *The Red Hat and the Cousin*, is breaking all box-office records. Its success proves that people need to go to the cinema to be entertained. They don't go to keep up with developments in the art of cinematography or to be preached at.

UC: Let's go back to your work with children . . .

AK: Working with children has helped me in my private life more than in my professional life. Children know less than adults but they have a healthier attitude to life. I've made the best possible deal with them: I've provided them with knowledge and they've brought me health. Children have taught me to live. They are budding mystics.

UC: The Chinese philosopher Lao-tze was nicknamed "the old child" . . .

AK: When I had a real problem I would put it to my younger son, who always had a magnificent answer. They have an answer to everything: "So what?" It's great. You present them with terrible disasters and they reply "So what?" You tell a child "Wrap up well or you'll catch cold" and he replies "So what?," "You'll get wet"—"So what?," "You'll have a temperature"—"So what?"

When times are hardest they answer your questions without hesitation. They stop what they're doing for a moment and come out with their "So what?," then go back to their game. Like the Sufi mystics, they take advantage of the moment, they live in the present, the here and now. I believe the definition of mystics also fits children. There are budding mystics all around us and we don't appreciate them.

UC: Apart from children, you like to work with nonprofessional actors, mostly from rural backgrounds. How much difference does appearing in a film make to their lives?

AK: Financially speaking, their situation is improved but you need to get very close to them to know how much they may have changed inside. Maybe it harms their ego, as some Iranian journalists have claimed—they become a focus of attention for a short while and then all of a sudden they are forgotten. But I have no choice in the matter, I can't re-engage the same children all the time. When I feel guilty about this, I try to imagine how I would feel in their shoes. Would I refuse a pleasant dream, knowing that when I awoke life's difficulties would still be there? No, I would be prepared to make the trip....

UC: What is the first image you remember seeing on film?

AK: The roaring Metro-Goldwyn-Mayer lion, in 1950, when I was ten. But I also played with bits of film when I was small. I thought they were stamps that had to be looked at against the light....

UC: How did you get into filmmaking?

AK: By chance. I studied at the Tehran Faculty of Fine Arts, designed advertising posters and illustrated children's books. In 1969 I was asked to do some work for the Institute for the Intellectual Development of Children and Adolescents. I worked with amateurs on my first film, *Bread and the Street* (1970) [later known as *Bread and Alley*]. It's the story of a child who buys some bread and wants to go home but is frightened by a dog in the street. We didn't have a child actor or a trained dog and I was a novice myself. We three non-professionals got together, and that became a kind of model for my later work.

A Fax Conversation between Jonathan Rosenbaum and Abbas Kiarostami

Jonathan Rosenbaum / 1997

From Jonathanrosenbaum.net, November 19–20, 1997. Reprinted by permission.

Fax sent by Jonathan Rosenbaum to Abbas Kiarostami, November 18, 1997

Dear Abbas (if I may),

I've been moved to write you this letter because of the distressing news I recently heard that you decided to delete the final sequence of *The Taste of Cherry* from the version of the film opening in Italy. I've also heard that there is a danger that you may cut the same sequence when the film opens in the United States. I must confess that when I heard this news, I experienced a painful feeling of loss—as if something I loved had suddenly been taken away from me. And I would like to try to persuade you not to touch a frame of your masterpiece.

I've seen *The Taste of Cherry* three times—twice in Cannes [in May 1997] and once in New York [in October 1997]—and although I consider it to be one of your finest works, with or without the video ending, I believe that only with the ending as it now stands does it possibly qualify as your greatest film. I won't attempt to explain all the reasons why I feel this way in a letter—although I will attempt to do so when the film comes to Chicago and I write about it in my newspaper. For now, I can only stress that I regard the ending as a very special gift to the audience—a gift that has complex and profound consequences in terms of how every viewer comes to terms with everything in the film preceding that ending. Without it in any way diminishing the remainder of the film, it allows it to reverberate in a wider, freer world, and allows the viewer to receive it in a fuller way. I should add that I don't think this opinion is merely an "American" or "Western" interpretation; [Iranian, Chicago-based teacher, writer, and filmmaker] Mehrnaz Saeed-Vafa, for example, fully agrees with me about the absolutely vital importance of the video ending. (I just spoke to her on the phone, and she asked me to tell you that she feels as passionately about this matter as I do.)

I realize that *The Taste of Cherry* is a deeply personal work for you, and I wouldn't presume to guess the reasons why the video ending troubles you. But I do believe that many of the greatest artists are capable of producing work that "understands" more than the artists sometimes do as individuals; that, I assume, is why Gogol destroyed the second half of his *Dead Souls* after writing it—because his novel in some mysterious fashion knew more than he did. Not knowing you, it would be foolish for me to speculate why you've had second thoughts about the ending of *The Taste of Cherry*. But I do feel that I know something about your work, and the wisdom it imparts to me is something I continue to listen to. I humbly ask you to listen to the same wisdom, and to allow it to speak to others.

Sincerely (and hopefully),
Jonathan Rosenbaum

Fax sent by Abbas Kiarostami to Jonathan Rosenbaum, November 20, 1997

Dear Jonathan (if I may),

I just returned from a long trip and got your fax. I do appreciate your concern and also your feeling on cinema and I . . .

As for the ending sequence, you are quite right and I have to say that I am not supposed to cut or change it at all, neither in my country or anywhere else. I just saw the dubbed version of my film in Italy and decided to play around the screening of the film with and without the video ending in several cities. Some theaters are showing the film with the video ending and some without. It's just a sort of playing, done out of the film . . . a play that you can see the audience reactions after two different endings . . . frankly speaking, I like this play . . . it's very interesting like cinema . . .

Life does worth to experience anything once. If I could ever find a chance to meet you, I'll tell you more in this respect.

Then, assure you again, the ending will be the same.
Thank you for your attention.

Sincerely,
Abbas Kiarostami
with regards to Mehrnaz

Jonathan Rosenbaum

A few words about the preceding: my letter wasn't prompted by any thoughts of publication, but simply by my alarm upon hearing, first, that many critics (Iranian as well as American) were trying to convince Kiarostami to delete his original ending from *Taste of Cherry* (which was still sometimes being called *The Taste of Cherry* at its festival showings), and second, that Kiarostami had done just that in Italy—which implied to me that he might do the same thing when the film opened in the US. It struck me as extraordinary that reviewers who see a film only once or twice could wind up as the final arbiters of works that filmmakers spent years working on, yet the recent and injurious recutting of other films prompted by reviews in trade magazines demonstrated that this practice was in fact on the rise.

It's worth adding that Italian screenings of the film without the ending proved to be more popular than screenings with the ending, and after Kiarostami left Italy, despite his wishes to have the film shown in both versions, the distributor opted to show only the cut version. (To the best of my knowledge, this shorter version hasn't been shown anywhere else in the world, but it's difficult to be sure about this.)

Prior to our exchange of faxed letters, my acquaintance with Kiarostami was limited. Saeed-Vafa had introduced us and served as interpreter during a brief conversation at the 1992 Toronto Film Festival, and subsequently we had merely nodded at one another at two or three other festivals, then conversed again briefly—with Mehrnaz again serving as interpreter—at the 1997 New York Film Festival in October. (Mehrnaz and I had worked together, along with a few others, on the English subtitles of Forugh Farrokhzad's only film, the 1962 short *The House Is Black*, which showed with *Taste of Cherry* at the festival.)

On February 28, 1998, Kiarostami presented two prerelease screenings of *Taste of Cherry* at the Chicago Art Institute's Film Center. In between those screenings, when I attended a dinner for Kiarostami, he asked me if my letter to him could be translated and printed in an Iranian film magazine, and I agreed, suggesting that perhaps his letter could be translated and printed as well. I later heard that my letter—though not his—appeared in Persian in *Film International*, and I've taken the liberty of reproducing Kiarostami's letter here verbatim because I believe that what it manages to communicate is far more important than his grasp of English grammar (which is certainly far superior to my nearly nonexistent knowledge of Farsi). The fact that we were able to communicate at all in this fashion is fundamental to my sense of what this book is about—in particular the sense of mutual empowerment that can arise from such exchanges.[1]

Note

1. To avoid possible confusion, in this sentence Jonathan Rosenbaum is not referring to this book, the one you are currently reading. His is a reference to his own work.

Between Dreams and Reality

UNESCO Courier / 1998

From *UNESCO Courier*, February 1998, pp. 48–50. Reprinted by permission of *UNESCO Courier*.

UNESCO Courier: How did you get into films?
Abbas Kiarostami: My roots were in graphic art; I branched out into cinema quite by chance. Graphic art is a kind of minimalist art in which one has to communicate an idea in a precise and agreeable form using great economy of means. I learned to live with the constraints of graphic art, and this helped me to accept constraints in general and use them in my films. My son wants to be a filmmaker but I have advised him to learn graphics first.

While I was a graphic artist, I started making advertising films as well. In advertising films, you have only thirty seconds or a minute to get a message across. You have to know your target audience very well: you have to know how people act and react: you have to know all about marketing. When you have to condense a message into one short minute, you learn what a minute really is. Making advertising films gave me an opportunity to learn all about filmmaking before getting into real cinema. Today I do everything in my films: I write the script, visualize the scenes with sketches, direct, supervise the sound and its mixing, choose the music and take care of the montage.

UC: What are the possibilities of cinema?
AK: To my mind cinema offers greater possibilities for self-expression than any other art. Absolutely anything can be depicted in cinema and this is not really possible in the other arts. In a film you can use silence or darkness, for instance, to great effect. At the end of my latest film, *The Taste of Cherry*, the central character, Mr. Badii, goes down into a pit and lies down. The moon disappears behind clouds and everything fades into darkness. For a whole minute nothing is shown on the screen. Life, cinema and light become one. With its magical power, cinema is a remarkable instrument for stimulating wonder and casting doubt on the most deeply rooted ideas.

UC: Are there any images or ideas you are not allowed to show when you make films in Iran?

AK: The kind of violent scenes that appear in movies all over the world are prohibited in the Iranian cinema, where it is also virtually impossible to make any reference to sexuality. Wherever in the world my films are set, I can never make any allusion to sex in them.

In Iran, you cannot hold your wife's hand in the street. In a movie, if a woman falls down in the street, she can only be helped up by another woman because touching is involved. And so if you see a woman tumble in an Iranian film don't be shocked if a man happens to be standing nearby but does nothing to help. It's not that he's unwilling to lift the woman back onto her feet but that he is not supposed to do so. Don't be shocked if you see a woman drowning in a swimming pool or a lake and a man is standing around doing nothing. He's not allowed to do anything. In real life maybe he would step in, but not in a movie. It's not that Iranian people are cold-blooded—it's just a limitation imposed on Iranian cinema. Don't be surprised if you see in an Iranian film a woman wake up in bed wearing her *chador*. In real life this is absurd, but in the cinema women have to wear a *chador* all the time. It is forbidden to show dancing and drinking alcohol—but not smoking—in the cinema.

To receive an exhibition permit in the 1980s, all films had to go through a four-stage process involving approval of the synopsis, script, cast and crew, and the final film. The situation has not changed much since then. Although political and social criticism is not unknown in films, care is taken not to displease the clerical establishment. Ironically, however, prohibitions of this kind have helped the Iranian cinema to achieve success internationally because it has always had to face the challenge of not showing certain things or finding inventive ways of expressing them. The pressure has slackened a little since the new government took over recently and one hopes that filmmakers will now have more freedom.

UC: Are Iranian films widely distributed outside Iran?

AK: I think Iranian cinema today is well placed internationally. Few countries from my part of the world make films that have the kind of worldwide distribution that ours have, not to speak of appreciation from international critics. Only recently Iranian filmmakers have won four prizes at international film festivals. My *The Taste of Cherry* won the Golden Palm Award at the Cannes Film Festival, Jafar Panahi's *Mirror* won the Golden Leopard at the Locarno Festival, and at the Montreal Festival Majid Majidi won first prize for direction, as well as four other awards, for his film *Children of Heaven*. Even more recently Parwiz Shahabazi won first prize in the young filmmaker category for his film *Traveller from the South* at the Tokyo Film Festival. This is something very new for Iran.

Compare our situation with that of China. China was on the verge of the same kind of breakthrough three years ago. But Chinese films were often produced in America and many Chinese filmmakers depended on American finance. These films were given an American-style treatment and lost their Chinese flavor: American financing changed the whole structure of Chinese films. Iranian cinema, on the other hand, may lack technical rigor, finance to mount expensive productions, and access to networks but it has one invaluable advantage—ideas. Besides, the fact that American films are not distributed in Iran is a blessing in disguise because it means that our film industry has been protected from stiff competition. What's more, the commercial success of high-quality Iranian films has led banks to offer long-term loans for film production, thus placing the industry on a more secular basis.

UC: The main character in *The Taste of Cherry* decides to take his life. How did you come to make a film about suicide?

AK: There were a number of reasons. Firstly, statistics show that very few suicide attempts are successful; in other words the desire to live is a lot more powerful than the desire to die. Secondly, all religions strongly disapprove of suicide and what is forbidden naturally attracts curiosity and is worth looking at closely. We should be free to ask the question: "Must I continue to live or not?"

Life is a choice and not a sentence, but often we do not realize this. When we accept life as a bundle of constraints we are actually making a choice. I want to tell people: if you choose to live, then do it well. So many people are standing by the exit door: they neither take part in life wholeheartedly nor leave it. They live in the shadow of death.

Let us not pass judgment on the act of suicide. It may be an act of violence, but in my film it is accompanied by critical enquiry. Mr. Badii wants to communicate with people; otherwise he could have quietly ended his life in bed by taking sleeping pills. But the really important thing is that life goes on, that there is an unending cycle in which nature sheds its old skin and grows a new one. This is more important than wanting to know whether a character is alive or dead at the end of the film.

Actually the film has more to do with life and death than with suicide and that is not a new subject for me. Three of my films—*Where Is the Friend's Home?* (1987), *And Life Goes On* (1992) and *Through the Olive Trees* (1991)—are shown as a trilogy because they were shot in the same location. But if you replace *Where Is the Friend's Home?* with *The Taste of Cherry*, it makes another trilogy whose theme is the fight for life and awareness of death, appreciating life and accepting responsibility for it while knowing that the exit door is just around the corner. The Romanian writer E. M. Cioran once said, "Without the possibility of suicide, I would have committed suicide quite a few years ago."

UC: Did you have problems dealing with this issue?

AK: It is true that in Iran suicide is forbidden by Qur'anic law. Catholics too are strongly opposed to suicide. But there are also other people in the world who are not religious, and besides, religious laws and those who uphold them may not always have respect for our lives. In Iran we have a religion with two parallel streams: one is devoid of the spirit of enquiry and flows backwards; the other is more developed and accepts enquiring minds.

UC: In your work the plot of one film often blends imperceptibly into that of another....

AK: Yes. This is particularly true of my latest trilogy in which each film emerges from the previous one much like a Russian doll. My films never tell a story which begins at one point and ends at another. A new story always begins somewhere along the way. And the stories are blended together to such an extent that it's impossible to separate them. In fact they are all part of a single story. Another thing: I think it's important that filmmakers should leave their films somewhat incomplete so that spectators can complete them using their own imagination.

UC: Nature is a constant presence in your films.

AK: Yes. We are separated from nature but we are part of it. Industrialization and progress have not really come to our rescue. To rediscover ourselves, we must go back to nature. In *The Taste of Cherry*, I tried to show the gradual encroachment of the industrial landscape and people's relation to it. Nature has been modified and destroyed by human hand and is being eaten up by expanding cities. The old taxidermist in the museum says to Mr. Badii: "Are you in despair? Have you never looked at the moon? Don't you want to see the stars? And the nights of the full moon? Don't you want to hear the whisper of the rain, the song of the nightingale? You want to close your eyes? My dear fellow, you should see all these things! Those who live in the other world want to come over here to see, and you want to hurry to go there?"

UC: What do you think of the violence that pervades cinema today?

AK: Violence, like kindness, is a part of human beings, and as long as it exists it is probably necessary to show it. But there is a difference between violence as it exists and violence as it is expressed in films. I think violence tends to be artificially treated in the cinema. The kind of violence that prevails in real life is cold, grey violence but it is shown in cinema in red-hot blood and guts form. We have seen so much of this fake violence that its so-called magic does not work anymore. But the merchants of violence go on making fortunes out of conjuring up a phantasm of this impulse that is inside everybody and rooted in society. For twenty years most mainstream cinema has not shown violence as it really is.

Violence was not treated like this in the past. In Fritz Lang's *The Big Heat* (1953), for example, it is completely internalized so that enormous tension is built up. The French director Claude Sautet's *Classe Tous Risques* (1960) also explored the psychology of violence with great skill and emotional realism. But what we see now is professional violence-mongering for its own sake. The irony is that nobody likes violence but everybody goes to see it.

UC: How do you feel about winning the Golden Palm at the 1997 Cannes Festival and UNESCO's Federico Fellini Gold Medal later in the year? Will these awards help your career?

AK: They certainly will. I am very proud and happy that such prizes have been awarded to my kind of cinema. The fact that such valuable awards are coming my way is very important because they encourage filmmakers to carry on producing "different cinema," cinema with a personal touch. They will attract audiences to come and see this kind of cinema and give it greater prestige. Good cinema cannot exist without an audience.

UC: Who are your favorite filmmakers?

AK: I like cinema which has roots in reality and yet also explores dreams. There are many filmmakers I like, but if I had to name one it would be Yasijiro Ozu of Japan.

UC: How should the cause of non-commercial cinema be defended today?

AK: Much commercial cinema is churned out in response to market forces. But this process contains the seeds of its own destruction because there is a limit to what people can take. The gap between this kind of cinema and the reality of normal life has become so great that people don't recognize themselves anymore in this kind of film.

There is not much to be done to counter this trend; it is going to self-destruct. I certainly hope that a different kind of cinema will come into its own and that real cinema will put a stop to fake cinema. To help this to come about, it is crucial that this new cinema should be given critical recognition.

Interview with Abbas Kiarostami for a Book by Jonathan Rosenbaum

Jonathan Rosenbaum and Mehrnaz Saeed-Vafa / 1998

From Jonathanrosenbaum.net, March 1, 1998. Reprinted by permission.

On March 1, the morning after Kiarostami presented *Taste of Cherry* at the Film Center, I arranged to meet him and Mehrnaz for a conversation over breakfast recorded specifically for *Movie Mutations*; Muhammed Pakshir, another Iranian living in Chicago, graciously drove us to the restaurant and joined us in part of the talk. Although it was mainly my intention at the time to discuss general issues about nationality and audiences, Kiarostami wound up explaining a great deal about his working methods—more than I had encountered in other interviews with him that I'd read at the time—and I've decided to retain portions of that material here.

Two subsequent interviews that Mehrnaz and I conducted with Kiarostami about his next two features for a book about him that we were cowriting are excerpted below to update some of his thoughts about interactive cinema, sound, nationality, and related matters. (Some parts of this material, I should add, don't appear in the aforementioned book.) Our hopes of interviewing him yet again about his latest feature, *10* (2002), which we managed to see just in time to add something to our book, were ultimately dashed by the increased difficulties imposed by US customs on Iranians entering the US after 11 September 2001—which even went beyond those described in "Squaring the Circle" elsewhere in *Movie Mutations*—understandably convinced Kiarostami to cancel a planned visit in the spring.

Mehrnaz Saeed-Vafa: Jonathan is preparing a book, and part of it will be this conversation with you.

Jonathan Rosenbaum: Its working title is *Movie Mutations: The Changing Face of World Cinema*. "Mutation" implies biological transformation, and the basic idea is that there are changes going on all over the world in communications, technology, and economics that are changing the ways we think and write about cinema. We want to have sections in the book about Iranian and Taiwanese cinema, and when Edward Yang was in town a few months ago we already began discussing some of the issues I want to bring up here. For me, part of what links Taiwanese cinema to Iranian cinema is a certain resistance to western values.

Abbas Kiarostami: Why Edward Yang and not Hou Hsiao-hsien, whose style is more distinctive?

JR: Because he was here. Of course I'd also like to include Hou in our discussion as well.

MS: Jonathan wants to emphasize how audiences are hungry for an alternative—for a different vision.

JR: And it's an interesting paradox that you're perceived in most of the world as an Iranian filmmaker, whereas in Iran you're perceived largely as a western filmmaker. How do you feel about this? What are the differences between the perceptions of your films in Iran and how they're perceived elsewhere? I was very much struck by something a Peruvian film critic said to me in Chicago about a year ago: he had recently seen Hou's *Goodbye South, Goodbye*, and he felt it had more to say to him about what's happening in Peru now than any other film made anywhere else.

AK: I feel the same way—that our language, Hou's and mine, is a universal language. And if film doesn't cross geographical borders, what else can? Everything else serves to preserve the borders and separations of cultures, customs, and nationalities. Film is the only way of looking down at cultures from a less earthbound perspective.

JR: Yes, but whenever one crosses a border, the idea of nationality appears. Perhaps economic matters are more important than national issues—which is why the Peruvian critic was affected by Hou's film: because people tearing down buildings and other manifestations of capitalism mattered more to him than the national differences between Taiwan and Peru.

AK: I also believe that Taiwan and Iran have many things in common—extraordinary similarities. And the most important of these are economic. Naturally, Iran is related to other countries through its economic situation, which is related to the political situation, and the political situation reflects the social situation. So all the countries with economic similarities have similar problems, which drives them to arrive at a common language.

I had a friend in Iran who was supposed to make a film in the United States, and he was afraid that if he was given a big budget, he wouldn't know how to spend the money and couldn't make a film according to his own standards. On the other hand, in Iran we sometimes don't have enough money to make films.

This kind of difference is the major disagreement between the cinemas of Iran and the United States. For example, if they invited me to make a film here and assigned me a big budget and a large crew, I'd have a lot of trouble making my own kind of film in those conditions.

JR: Raúl Ruiz hated making *The Golden Boat* in New York, because so many film students wanted to work with him as assistants and his crew became so large. But part of how that system operates in the US is through unions. Are there unions of the same kind in Iran?

AK: Yes, in every part of the profession, but they don't enforce their regulations so much, so you can still have a crew of less than ten people.

I think this changing taste in cinema all over the world partly stems from economic factors, but there are other important factors as well. One of the most important is a participating audience that is active, not passive. The filmmakers themselves aren't the only spokespeople; spectators also have the role and the right to create part of the film. Just because they don't have access to the negative and the film equipment doesn't mean that they don't deserve to be regarded as part of the film. I believe the present distance between the filmmaker and the audience is immense, and my kind of filmmaking is interested in reducing that distance. There are definitely people in the audience who are every bit as talented as I am or even more, and they should be given the opportunity to be creative and become part of the filmmaking.

It seems to me like there is only one audience everywhere I go, and I've learned a great deal from this significant similarity of audiences. I feel like I'm always in the same situation with the audience, and that there's a similarity to their reactions, despite differences in nationality, religion, origin, culture, and language. For instance, when I was showing *Through the Olive Trees* in Taipei, I completely forgot that the audience there wasn't Iranian. I had a similar experience in Rotterdam with *Homework*, an even more local film. I thought at first this was because there were some Iranians in the audience, but when the lights came on I discovered there weren't any. I think all people are impressed by film in similar ways.

Muhammed Pakshir: I think what he's trying to accomplish is the elimination of the separation between one filmmaker and thousands of spectators, and that's a big achievement.

JR: Yes, and part of the way you're achieving this in *Taste of Cherry* is by being multicultural. Someone pointed out at the Film Center last night that the three major characters apart from the hero are Afghan, Kurdish, and Turkish, and as you pointed out, that's because Iran itself is multicultural. This is already a step in the direction you're talking about, because what we're calling "Iran" is in fact many cultures, not one—just as "America" is.

AK: And none of these cultural differences interferes with the film being understood. Spectators check their cultural baggage at the door, before they enter the theater; this is the way that audiences are similar.

JR: It seems that part of what makes your films so interactive is the fact that there are almost always missing parts of the narrative—absences that the audiences have to fill in some way.

AK: My ideal film is something like a crossword puzzle with empty squares that the audiences can fill in. Some people describe films as flawless, without cracks, but for me that means that an audience can't get inside them.

MS: Did you inform the actors in *Taste of Cherry* when you were shooting and when you were just rehearsing?

AK: No. There was no film crew there. They would set up the camera for me in the car, because I was the only one around apart from the actor [i.e., serving as the stand-in for the character the actor was speaking or listening to].

JR: Did the actors have to memorize their lines?

AK: Nothing was written, it was all spontaneous. I would control certain parts and get them to say certain lines, but it was basically improvisation.

JR: So were all these actors speaking as themselves?

AK: Not exactly. The actor playing the soldier wasn't a soldier; I prompted him beforehand about the location of the army camp, for example. It was a combination of real and unreal. For instance, I ordered some guns, so he thought he'd get a chance to shoot one of them later on, when we were filming, and he didn't realize that this kind of instruction was the actual filming. He was even getting anxious and asking when the filming would start. I actually made him believe I was planning to kill myself.

It reminds me of a verse from the poet Rumi: "You are like the ball I hit, so you are running, but I am also running after you."

JR: It seems to have something in common with jazz. Maybe that's why I like your use of Louis Armstrong playing "St. James Infirmary" in the final sequence.

AK: Exactly. Because even though you're following certain notes, you're also following the feeling of the piece, so the performance you're giving tonight will be different from the performance tomorrow.

JR: It's also about playing together.

AK: Yes, but these actors can't have a dialogue with each other because one part is always played by me.

JR: Right—you're the composer and the bandleader.

AK: At one point, I wanted the soldier character to express amazement, but since I couldn't ask him to do that, I started to speak to him in Czech. He said he couldn't understand what I was talking about, and I used that in the film. At another point, I placed a gun in the glove compartment, and asked him to open it for a chocolate, when I wanted him to look afraid.

JR: One thing that *Taste of Cherry* conveys very powerfully is the experience of being alone, and your method of shooting intensifies that sense of isolation.

AK: There are signs in the film that sometimes made me think that the man didn't really want to kill himself, that he was looking for a kind of communication with the other characters. Maybe that's one of the ruses of his loneliness, to engage people with his own emotional issues. He doesn't pick up a couple of workers at the beginning who would be willing to kill him with their spades; he chooses other people whom he probably thinks he can have a conversation with. So that gives us a signal that he's probably not searching for someone who would help him to kill himself.

JR: It's also interesting how your images metaphorically reproduce the situation of the spectator watching the film. In many of your films, the view through a car's windshield represents that situation—of looking for something but also feeling separate from what you're looking at.

AK: That comes from my experience of driving around Tehran in my car and sometimes driving outside the city—looking through the front, rear, and side windows, which become my frames.

Nature Has No Culture: The Photographs of Abbas Kiarostami

Shiva Balaghi and Anthony Shadid / 2000

From *Middle East Report*, no. 219, Summer 2001. Interview conducted in April 2000. Reprinted by permission.

The notes below are part of the original article and not additions by the editor of this book.

In April 2000, Abbas Kiarostami received the Akira Kurosawa Lifetime Achievement Award at the San Francisco Film Festival. While in the United States, Kiarostami visited New York City, where the Andrea Rosen Gallery mounted the first US exhibition of Kiarostami's photographs. The photographs, which were shown in a stark white loft space, appeared without titles, dates or labels. Anthony Shadid and Shiva Balaghi spoke with Kiarostami about his art photography.

A battered SUV rumbles across a country road, winding through wheat fields. We hear a conversation between the passengers, who are trying to decipher the vague driving directions they've been given for finding a small village tucked in the hillside. They are to take a turn just beyond the solitary tree. As they drive along, they pass a majestic free-standing tree, its branches sprawled against a crisp cloudless sky. Moments later, they pass another solitary tree—and then another and another. Which of these trees marks the spot, they wonder? So begins Abbas Kiarostami's latest film, *The Wind Will Carry Us* (1999). Perhaps more than any other, this Kiarostami film treats the Iranian countryside as a character and not a placid backdrop. The landscapes—the contrasting colors of earth and sky, the stalks of wheat delicately moving to the breeze, the trees dotting the hillside—appear in characteristically long, uncut wide shots.

The title of the film is taken from the poetry of Forugh Farrokhzad and in a pivotal scene of the film, Forugh's poem is recited. A leading feminist poet who rose to prominence in the 1960s, Forugh drew on nature to construct strikingly visual metaphors describing the complexities of her quest for independence as a woman writer in Iran. At times, she depicted herself in her poetry as enclosed and detached, watching the world through the frame of a window. Yet Forugh's most evocative statement of intellectual and personal growth came in a verse where she exclaimed that she would plant her hands in the garden and grow. In Forugh's writings, nature and the garden, common tropes in classical Persian poetry, came to represent the elemental quality of gender politics, the unnaturalness of restrictions on women's lives.

Kiarostami draws on and extends Forugh's interpretation of nature in both his film and photographs.

The photographs exhibited in Manhattan in spring 2000 echo scenes from *The Wind Will Carry Us*. Though they are not film stills or location shots, Kiarostami said there is little difference between his filmmaking and photography. In the end, he sees their qualities merging.

"The nature that is in the location of my films can be seen in my photography, and I want my films to become closer to my photography and more distant from storytelling," he said. "It is true that these are completely separate milieus, but in my opinion, the ideal situation for me is for these two areas—photography and cinema—to become closer to one another." Long before he began his career as a filmmaker, Kiarostami trained as a painter in the School of Fine Arts at Tehran University. He went on to work as a graphic artist and as a commercial director. In 1969, one of his commercials caught the eye of Firuz Shirvanlu, the director of the Center for the Intellectual Development of Children and Young Adults. Kiarostami was asked to establish a film division at the center. In 1970, he produced his first film, a short entitled *Bread and Alley*.[1] Since then, Kiarostami has directed nearly thirty films and has come to the attention of some of the leading figures of world cinema.[2] Akira Kurosawa has said, "When Satyajit Ray passed on, I was very depressed. But after seeing Kiarostami's films, I thanked God for giving us just the right person to take his place."[3]

In his films, Kiarostami has explored the relationship between fiction and reality, the subjectivity of truth as framed by the camera's lens. Resisting a comfortable narrative, Kiarostami challenges the viewer to engage with his films, rather than to view them passively. Photography, which he took up during the revolution at a time that he doubted his future as a filmmaker, offers him another way to interact with his audience; they are called on to actively participate in the generation of meaning in Kiarostami's art.[4]

"I prefer the gaze of a viewer in front of a photograph to the kind of gaze that an audience of my films has in a theater," Kiarostami said. "The expectation of a viewer in the theater is to look for the continuities and changes in a story. He has grown accustomed to sitting in a theater and listening to a story. But in a gallery, I have seen that the viewers look at each single photograph, their gaze is more focused on the photograph, because they do not expect to hear a story." Like his films, his photographs are presented without expected guideposts that explain their significance. There are no labels, no titles, no dates. It is left to the viewer to lend them a particular meaning. Though it may appear that his lens reveals an unchanging and placid nature, Kiarostami's photographs, in fact, seem to reveal a deeply political use of the landscape. "Photographs of nature are universal," he said. "A tree has no ethnicity, no birth certificate, no passport, no nationality, therefore what difference does it make where in the world this tree is? What is important is the similarity between all trees, the similarity between all skies, the similarity between all landscapes. Nature has no specific culture. I am emphasizing this lack of ethnicity of nature. Therefore I do not want to mark the specific time and place of my photographs."

Some themes emerge in his photographs—the solitary tree, for instance. Kiarostami acknowledges the pattern, but assigns a random, incidental quality to it. "I did not know that there would be a theme found in my photographs at a later stage," he said. "I know that each solitary tree, if it had a particular purity, invited me to stop and take its photograph. I did not plan to have so many solitary trees in my photographs over the years. But each of these trees has its own purity, its own individuality. I may have passed by a tree time and again over the years and never photographed it; one day it may invite me to stop and take its picture. If there is a theme, it has developed over the years."

By chronicling what he sees, Kiarostami said he views himself as a journalist, in a sense. His intervention, he said, is crucial to capture a moment in time. "A photojournalist covers the news from the scene of war, and I, with nature, cover the news of the scene of peace. I don't think there is a fundamental difference; it is a difference in the selection of a subject. For a photojournalist, a moment is important—the moment for taking a photograph. For a photographer of nature, this particular moment is also important. Without those moments, no image is worth recording. There is only one moment in which a photograph can be taken."

Since the 1980s, when his films were first shown outside of Iran, Kiarostami has achieved a growing reputation as a filmmaker in the West. When asked if he sees a difference in his role as an artist within Iran as opposed to an artist producing for a Western audience, Kiarostami offers an emphatic response that signals the clearly political quality of the universality in his nature photographs. "No, in a sense, this is a question that has its answer in it. You ask me this question but know my answer. In my mind a human being has a universal quality. If there has been a division of humanity into smaller groups, it is because of economic and political conditions. And the framework of cultural conditions that exist are influenced by economics and politics. But mankind must be a universal being. It is my ambition that each person see themselves as a human being first and not as an ethnicity. These classifications occurred later, in my opinion. A person is not born with a birth certificate, with a passport. When you speak about a human being, and not about his culture or his nationality or his politics, naturally, you can communicate with all of the people of the world. And for this reason, each person who speaks at a profound level of humanity can be understood by anyone. Without nationality, language, tribalism and culture, all people are the same."

Notes

The authors would like to thank Abbas Kiarostami, Jamsheed Akrami, and Andrea Rosen.

1. For more on the history of the Center's activities, see Saeed Sharifi, "The Center for Intellectual Development of Children and Young Adults, 1965–1996," Goftego (Spring 1998). Translated into English at www.netiran.com.
2. For a complete filmography, consult www.imdb.com.
3. From the official website for the film Taste of Cherry, www.Zeitgeistfilm.com/currenc/tasteofcherry/kiarostami.html. Kiarostami won numerous prestigious awards, including the Palme D'Or at the Cannes Film Festival in 1997 for *Taste of Cherry*. The same year, he received the UNESCO Fellini Medal in Gold for his achievements in film, freedom, peace and tolerance.
4. Casey Williamson, "Art Matters: The Films of Abbas Kiarostami," in Rose Issa and Sheila Whitaker, eds., *Lift and Art: The New Iranian Cinema* (London: Visiting Arts, 1999).

Meeting Abbas Kiarostami—
The 24th Montreal World Film Festival

Peter Rist / 2000

From *Offscreen*, vol. 5, no. 2, March 2001. Interview conducted in summer/fall 2000. Reprinted by permission of *Offscreen* and Peter Rist. Interpreter and translator: Shahin Parhami. Additional translation by Afshin Tarbiyat.

Annotations within the interview below are part of the original print. No additions were made by the editor of this book.

The cinephilic city of Montreal was blessed with the presence of Abbas Kiarostami, who was invited as head of the film jury for the 2000 24th Montreal World Film Festival. The festival also paid hommage to Kiarostami with a retrospective of nine feature films. *Offscreen* thanks the festival for inviting one of the grand masters of contemporary cinema and making the following interview possible.

Peter Rist: The very first film of yours that I saw was in 1992, the English title of which is *And Life Goes On*, and I knew from the very first shot that I was watching something totally original, perhaps unique, so, I wanted to ask a question about the way you shoot perpendicularly to the action at 90 degrees. In this first shot we are looking at a tollbooth and cars are going by, and then for the rest of the film, predominantly, we are travelling in a car and the camera is looking at 90 degrees to the landscape, the people and the houses, and I wondered about how the camera frame seems like a window on the world, but also functions like a mask, so if you could just talk a little bit about that kind of style . . .

Abbas Kiarostami: My approach to cinema is according to the situation that exists. This is a spontaneous process and I have not thought of it in advance. *And Life Goes On* was my own actual experience. It was the third day of the earthquake in Iran when my son and I went to see what had happened to the kids who had acted in my film. Therefore, I think my first mental image of making this film is the reality and my one-day trip to the earthquake-stricken areas. I think it is the idea that dictates the form. I always believe that when one has the content in mind, the form is created without much thinking. I mean once the film has been shot, I can see what kind of style I have chosen.

PR: Yes, I am obviously interested in the "content" of your films, also, and I am only asking questions like this because I'm very struck by the originality of the style, and how it does change as well from film to film. For example, in *The Taste of Cherry*, you will use a car, which is different because you are always going up and down hills, and the landscape is changing in interesting ways, so sometimes it is very barren, and eventually you are amongst vegetation. My experience of watching your films is that I am so fascinated by what I am looking at, so to me, the cinematography is part of the essence of your work.

AK: It is your perception of the film that can help you find the differences of style in my films. As a filmmaker, a distance of five years separates the two films and it is for this reason that I say I, too, have to watch the film as a viewer, because I do not watch my own films. I have made these films and for me they lack the same originality that you find in them. For me to realize whether there is a difference in the way these two films ask questions, I have to put them side by side and compare them. The way you view the film is yours or perhaps a mix of your view and the film but not necessarily the film's own point of view.

There is definitely a reason for choosing to shoot any given scene in a specific manner in my films. When you choose, it means that you disregard other possible choices. So, there has to be a concrete reason. Perhaps if you have any specific scene in mind, I can talk about that . . .

PR: OK. For example, in your most recent film, the title *The Wind Will Carry Us* which I know is the title of a poem, and this is very important in terms of the film, but, at the beginning of the film I am so struck not by "wind" but by the earth, by gravity . . . a children's ball bounces down a hill and the camera is following the ball, and then water is running down . . . , but the central character always has to go to the top of the mountain (which is very funny, I think) in order to hear his cell phone, so for me "gravity," actually is the force which seems to be driving the film initially . . . Again, this is my "reading" . . .

AK: You can always find similarities between films. Some people point out, for example, graphic elements in a shot or actions, for example in *Where Is the Friend's House?*, you see the kid climbing the hill to reach his friend [as a challenge?]. Someone else's reading is that this is similar to the man climbing the mountain again in *The Wind Will Carry Us* but this time, here, it is towards death (marked by the cemetery) although the action is almost the same. I did not have this connection in mind consciously, after ten or fifteen years between making these two films. But I believe these choices take place at an unconscious level for each film.

PR: I didn't realize, the first time I saw *The Wind Will Carry Us*, that it took place in Kurdistan. I knew I was seeing a different landscape and a different culture, but in this film and in the previous film, *The Taste of Cherry*, you are dealing with marginal characters from other ethnic groups. For example, in *Cherry*, I think that every person who gets in the car is from a different ethnic group, and I thought... People are always asking questions on politics in Iranian films, but, to me, this was very subtle inclusion of politics. The very fact that these characters were from other ethnic groups, it is not obvious what you are saying about outsiders but all of these "outsider" people are helping this man. I found this curious too, so, what am I asking well, Is there a very subtle political subtext in these two films based on ethnicity?

AK: Not in the customary way of political films. The political films are the ones that try to replace a regime with another one. With this definition, my films are not political films at all. The real political films deal with social issues, concern the social/political landscape that one lives in, and thus are based on reality. However, I have a strong feeling against films which are "ideologically" political and lose their function in a short period. The real political truth can be found in films that don't claim to be "political." But I can't say if these two films are political or not. First we should define politics, and find out how the viewer defines politics as well, and then we can discuss if the film can be categorized as a political film.

PR: Well, I'm glad that you've said that with regards to the "ideologically" political film. I think that in a human sense, even though there are bad or negative things happening in your films, there's always a movement towards a kind of a positive thread, that is again subtle and not obvious. In this particular case in *The Taste of Cherry*, I felt it was in the relationships with these "foreigners" which actually helped the man feel more positive about life. No, it's not political because no one is going to make a political analysis of that, but it is a kind of "human politics."

It struck me that *The Traveller* is like the *Citizen Kane* of the Iranian children's cinema, or something, it seems like a blueprint for so many other films that have been made in the last twenty years involving children in Iranian cinema. Is this the way this film is discussed in Iran, is it regarded as being...

AK: It was the first middle-length film made in Iran with this kind of subject, some twenty-eight years ago.

PR: I was even surprised at the boy running all the time, which is not typical in your films, but is very typical now in other Iranian films.

AK: I think "running" is a character of the East and not necessarily Iran. The Easterners or the people of the third world have to work much harder than other nations. But if we really want to consider the meaning of these lives, this running is neither futile nor devoid of reason. They don't have a choice and that is a reality itself. This view encompasses not only the children but also the adults. Right now, most Iranians work three jobs. We even have an expression in Farsi "running like a dog" which means working hard in order to make ends meet.

PR: I had seen Naderi's *The Runner*, which I had always thought was a great film, but I didn't realize that there was a precedent in your work. I had always thought of him as being the other Iranian director apart from yourself who was an original stylist, but even Naderi was influenced by you.

AK: I actually started my career as a filmmaker before Naderi, and in any case, this situation [of running] is a national one.

Abbas Kiarostami—The Poetry of Everyday Life

Mazzino Montinari / 2002

From Cineuropa.org, November 22, 2002. Reprinted by permission.

Following its premiere in Cannes and being released in France, Belgium and the United Kingdom, Abbas Kiarostami's new film, *Ten*, is about to be released in Italy. The Batìk Film Festival in Perugia is holding a retrospective of this Iranian director's work beginning on 21 November. Kiarostami is one of the living legends of world cinema; an expert in portraying everyday life and giving it universal appeal despite the critics who accuse Kiarostami of making films as stylistic exercises for fans of all things exotic.

Ten is based on a narrative structure that portrays facts that are valid for every single human being on this earth. The location is a car, the protagonists, five women and a child. Ten characters alternate between ten sequences. They talk with each other about their lives. There is no real storyline that unites the parts into a unit. And faced with this exhibition of reality, the spectator tries to reconstruct and link the events. Tiny fragments in which the women talk about marriage, divorce, betrayal, religion, sex and much else besides. *Ten* was never screened in Iran because the censor ordered Kiarostami to cut thirty minutes. As well as talking about this film, Kiarostami addressed the issue of European cinema and its financial problems. They, he believes, are the reason for the current stagnation and what has stopped cinema developing as an art.

Cineuropa: Your films are also co-produced by European companies. What is your relationship with Europe from the economic point of view?

Abbas Kiarostami: Many of my films were funded by Europeans as well as others. All the same, that is just a detail that I consider to be of secondary importance, in the sense that when I make a film, I only take care of the artistic aspects of the process. When filming is complete, I delegate others to find the money in Europe. I work in total independence. I am an independent director who follows his own personal path. I don't even worry about how many people will actually go and see the film. I am only too well aware of the fact that my films are light years away from their European and American counterparts in terms of spectacle and action. And so I know that the audience may well find a feature like *Ten* less appealing. You must however remember that ten seconds of *Star Wars* cost as much as one of my films so I don't try to make films that will lose money and remain free to experiment and try to find alternative cinematographic solutions. Moreover, with *Ten*, I used DV. That allowed me to keep costs down and have a smaller crew. All the actors are amateurs. The point I'm making is that money and production does not influence the genesis or the execution of my films. The important thing is having the courage to experiment and to take risks without being intimidated by the fact that only three people may go to see my film. Unfortunately, from the artistic point of view, cinema—when compared to disciplines like painting or music—has stalled. Too much depends on money. And Europe, like the US, has accepted to transform cinema into a mere monument for entertainment.

Cineuropa: You recently experienced problems with the Mexican authorities when they failed to issue you with a visa to visit New York for the presentation of *Ten*. Putting the political issue to one side for a moment, does this totally unjustified hostility encourage you to distinguish between the US and Europe where you have always received a warm and positive reception?

AK: All I want to say from the political point of view is that my personal case is not so important if we examine the context in which it took place. Even if Bush were a huge film fan and loved my work and had known that I cannot be compared to the Fundamentalist, I would still never ever had gotten the visa. We are at war and no exceptions are possible. As far as cinema is concerned, the distinction I make is between independent directors and those who are not independent. Unfortunately, the American point of view prevails and even Europeans are subject to it. There are few filmmakers who can work in conditions of total freedom, and it's got nothing whatsoever to do with nationality. Moretti and Angeloupoulos are amongst the handful of directors who really make independent films, but they are not the only ones. There are people in China and even in the US who do too.

Interview: Abbas Kiarostami

Ulrich Köhler and Benjamin Heisenberg / 2003

From Revolver-film.com, November 17, 2003. Reprinted by permission. Translated by Monika Raesch.

Revolver: [What led to this quote?] "If homeowners married homeowners, the rich married the rich, and the illiterate married the illiterate, nothing would work. Much better if the literate marry the illiterate, the rich marry the poor, and those with houses marry those without. That way they can all help each other out. If two people marry and end up with two houses, they can't live with their heads in one and their feet in the other." Is this Kiarostami speaking or is it the voice of Hossein, the protagonist of *Through the Olive Trees*?

Abbas Kiarostami: Both. I don't write any script until I have cast my actors. Of course, I have an idea, but I don't write them down. I use this idea to find an actor. And when I have found the right person who interests me, then I spend several months with them to get to know them. I travel with them and so on. Spending time together results in me also sharing my thoughts and ideas with these people. But I never say to my cast that these thoughts, that our conversations, should become dialogue in my movies. During this time together we do draft the dialogue without the actor knowing that we do so. These are basically the rehearsals. This definitely applies to the quote that you mentioned. Hossein and I drove somewhere together, and I asked him about the topic of marriage. I said to him: "Don't you think that it is better when rich live together with poor, when the educated live together with the uneducated. An exchange occurs in such situations and that's good." Basically, I put these thoughts in his mouth. But I didn't tell him that this thought should be part of the film; for him our conversation was a private one. In the evening, when we were together with the [film] crew, I told them that Hossein said something wonderfully philosophical. I asked Hossein to repeat the sentence from earlier in the day. He couldn't remember. I jumped in and repeated the thought, but credited Hossein with its origin. He was unsure whether he had truly said that, but felt honored. The DP [director of photography] praised him for his wisdom and told my former assistant [director Jafar Panahi] that same night that Hossein had said something very nice. My DP requested that Hossein repeat the sentence. Now, Hossein could remember it. The same evening, he repeated the sentence three or four more times to other people. Now the sentence was stuck in his head. Unbeknownst to him, he had just rehearsed for the film. The next day, he told the sentence to as many people as he could, including the driver. By now, he had convinced himself that this was his original idea. The evening prior to shooting the scene, we kept Hossein from sleeping. In the early morning hours, he was permitted to lie down for a little bit in the production van, but was not permitted to sleep. We set up the camera; he was called, and we requested that he sit down in front of the camera. I asked him to repeat his philosophical thought. He had repeated the sentence so many times that we only needed one take. It was perfect. The idea had completely become his own. Later, in interviews, he claimed that the sentence was his.

Revolver: Socialism was planted.

AK: Yes. My experience working with nonprofessional actors means that no script, no paper can be exchanged. If I were to hand someone a printed paper, they would automatically feel transported back to school. He would have the impression to have to memorize lines. And they object to that immediately: "No, we can't do that. We can't remember that." Even if they could remember, it would not have become their own [thought]. That is revealed by our eyes and gestures. We observe how they recite lines without realizing their content. The fictional scenario becomes unbelievable. That's why I developed other methods. I write down notes the evening before [a shoot], but don't bring paper or pen onto the set. We prepare by me reciting the dialogue, but I don't give time for the actor to memorize the lines. We continue talking about other matters, so that he forgets what I said. The actor only has some rough memory of what was said, but forgets the wording. When we shoot, he is forced to put the idea into his own words. That's how it becomes believable in front of a camera. Most thoughts are mine. But I can't transfer them directly onto a cast member. He understands the idea behind what I said, but adapts it using his own experience and language. That's when it gets interesting. Applying an idea to one's own life experience results in believability. Even though he may make an error, say something differently to what I had said before, whatever he says is much more believable and interesting than I what I said.

Revolver: How does this apply to Sabzian in your film *Close-Up*? It appears that some [nonprofessional] actors or protagonists bring more of themselves into the role than others.

AK: That applies to Sabzian. But even then, if one does not direct the performers, if one would not pay attention to [plot] continuity, if one were to let them do whatever they envision, then the story would fall apart. [The director] needs to find the connections and explain them to the actors; then they find their way. That's similar to [the sport of] polo. As the leader, you make the first move and then you have to follow the rolling ball. Propel the ball and follow it. You select the direction, but how many pushes the ball needs and what goal you hit, that's determined by others.

Revolver: Directors like Mike Leigh or Ken Loach were accused of providing a speculative perspective of the working class, since they belong to the middle class, even when providing authenticity . . .

AK: I view this accusation as unfounded and without merit. If it is an accusation against me, I would have to object to it. Also in regard to other directors, it doesn't make sense.

Revolver: All your films feature a character from Tehran's middle class, an educated person, who approaches a person from a different social standing. This character is somewhat of a representative [of the middle class]. The characters portraying directors in *Through the Olive Trees*, *The Wind Will Carry Us*, and *And Life Goes On*, and the photographer in *Ten*. They all portray someone else from their own social class. Their perspective looking in from the outside remains transparent. This is one way your films differ from those of Ken Loach, for example.

AK: One person works in one way, another works in another way. A person from the working class has to focus on matters that make it difficult to reflect on one's own life. What is wrong with an Übercapitalist such as Engels speaking up for the working class?[1] Important is a story's credibility, that one is genuinely interested in the people one portrays. Ermanno Olmi, Ken Loach, and I are planning a film to be shot in Italy.[2] The story plays on a train, in first class. Ken Loach asked us whether you could tell something about other people on the train because he didn't know how to relate to the people in first class. He doesn't have to. I have no problem with that. His imagination goes in one direction; he imagines how people sit on the roof of the train and ride it without a ticket. We will attempt to integrate such characters. Ken will work with those, and we [Ermanno and Abbas] will work with the others.

Revolver: There is a break between *The Wind Will Carry Us* and *ABC Africa*. I got the impression that that wasn't only about video production work, but also about self-awareness as a director. Were you concerned about method?

AK: I don't see that much of a difference. The themes, the stories of *The Wind Will Carry Us* and of *ABC Africa* are very similar. Working with a digital camera was new. It permitted me to work simpler, more precise and to-the-point. One additional big difference with *ABC Africa* was the lack of mise-en-scene; basically, the director was not present. The only important thing was the story that was being told. For me, *ABC Africa* is my most important film. [Working with] video was liberating. Since we had only traveled to Uganda with digital cameras for preproduction research, we didn't have to focus on the formal qualities of camera settings.[3] We only viewed [what we were shooting] as preproduction. When we wanted to prepare the actual shoot in Tehran, we watched the material and realized that it was completely unnecessary to return to Uganda. What we were able to capture on the digital cameras would have been impossible to record on a 35 mm camera and a large film crew.

I experienced such a liberating feeling for the first time in the closing sequence of *Taste of Cherry*. We had shot the ending on 35 mm, but it was destroyed in the development lab. We lost the material in its entirety. We couldn't reshoot, since by then spring had passed and the blossoms had fallen from the trees, the grass was yellow, and we didn't want to wait until next spring. That's why I used the material my son had shot. He had joined the shoot with a digital camera. For example, the scene with the soldiers: I realized that they were much more relaxed in front of his camera than they had been in front of mine. The impact of a large 35 mm camera inhibited them. Somehow I had forgotten about this experience. One forgets. Then, for *ABC Africa* this camera recommended itself to me again. It spoke to me and said, "Please, please work with me." When I was shooting *Ten*, I said to it: "I want you." A film such as *Ten* could have never been shot without the usage of a digital camera. The car is such a small, confined space; you can only work with video. The play was uninhibited and intense. I sat in the back of the car and did not interfere. I never called "cut." That happened in the editing room. They [the actors] didn't even realize when I made critical facial expressions, since I sat in the back of the car. I didn't sit there as a critic. I felt very free.

Revolver: Looking at your other films, they incorporate a philosophy of omissions,[4] in the visual and the dialogue. In the way something is being said or not being said. This philosophy must have something to do with expensive 35 mm film. This is completely different with video. What changed? Will this also impact mise-en-scene in the future?

AK: I will shoot my next film on 35 mm. There are films that must be shot on 35 mm; but there are also films that can only be shot on video. Mise-en-scene exists on video as well, but only emerges in the editing room. The director automatically becomes the screenwriter who sees everything; he is present, but doesn't have to take care of all the things he would have to worry about when shooting on 35 mm. Deciding between shooting on 35 mm and on video depends on the film's content and workflow.

Revolver: But it is also a question about sensuality?

AK: Of course. The question is a cost-benefit analysis. Each format has its own aesthetic, its own language. A painter has to decide whether he paints with oil or utilizes other materials. Either option has its own aesthetic value. Tonight, for instance, I will screen a short film from a series, five planned sequences.[5] It's obvious that I could have never shot these films on 35 mm. One of these shots is seventeen minutes long. You would never have the courage to shoot something like that on 35 mm. Like a large shadow, the producer is always hovering behind the director's back. 35 mm limits choices. With a video camera, you have to discover a new language. If we seize the opportunities video provides, then there is no difference, artistically speaking. Important is the emotion we bring to the work. If we have the right emotion, then we will also find the right language. Of course, I am aware of 35 mm fetishists. I am like that when it comes to photography. If someone says to me, "Use a digital camera," then I reply, "No, thank you, but no; I can't work with that. I need to experience the process of developing the print." I know that in a few years, the dark room will have become obsolete, and digital photography will have become dominant. Perhaps I am only a fanatic supporter of traditional photography because I just purchased an expensive Leica camera. [*Laughs*] The development of technology will bring new opportunities, completely new themes. I heard the singing of the frogs, and I used this camera to film the frogs. To me, the digital camera is like a visa into the free world.

Revolver: Are you still watching new films?

AK: I hardly go to the cinema. Or phrased better: I don't watch every movie. I only watch those films that have themes that interest me or were made by a director to whom I feel connected. I am an older man; I don't have to watch everything. I select. A very good friend of mine is an architect; but I know one thing, if he praises a film, then the film isn't actually good. That's a big help for me [in deciding what movies to watch]. I am very thankful. When he recommends something, I know I can skip watching that film. I carefully consider what I spend my finite time on.

I read philosophy and poetry, but not prose. I can't stand it when someone needs multiple pages to explain something, such as that the winter is over, and needs again multiple pages to elucidate that spring is nearing. I only need the first letter of the word spring to understand that. I read the first letter of the word mother and know that it's about a mother. I don't need an explanation that spans multiple pages. That's why I hate novels. In Iran, it does happen that due to faulty telephone connections, you suddenly listen into the conversation of two strangers. I happened to be present as two people conversed. I enjoy that much more than reading a novel. Such a telephone conversation is refreshing; you learn a lot; you learn about people. Novels, in contrast, are insulting; they are truly unworthy to the human race; they explain the tiniest shitty detail, as if the reader is too dumb to follow the plot otherwise.

Revolver: Do you have a particular novel in mind?

AK: Not in particular. I was speaking generally. Novelists like to be teachers. The time of the novel, the time of telling a story is over. That's how I see it. In contrast, poetry is very important to me. Forthcoming, a book of mine will be published by Suhrkamp Verlag.[6] My poems have four, five words. A novel is like a Bollywood film; everything gets explained.

Revolver: Is it true that you and Martin Karmitz [the French co-producer of all of Kiarostami's films since *Close-Up*] only shake hands to seal a deal?

AK: We don't even shake hands; we speak on the phone. I just deliver the finished film to him. Up to this point, there has never been a problem. I can't stand to have the shadow of the producer looming behind my back. That's because even I don't know what my finished film will look like [while I am in the process of shooting it]. As you know, I work without a formal script. I think there are only few producers who give this kind of freedom to directors. He watched *Close-Up*, tracked me down and told me that he feels he understands me, mentally speaking, and he has proven this over the past decade.

Notes

The interview was conducted in Berlin on November 17, 2003, by Ulrich Köhler und Benjamin Heisenberg. Interpreter: Huschang Kiarostami. Thank you: Renate Schubert/Akademie der Künste, Berlin.[7]

1. Friedrich Engels (1820–1895) was a German philosopher, historian, political scientist, and socialist. He coauthored the *Communist Manifesto* with Karl Marx, among other works.
2. Kiarostami is referring to what would eventually be the film *Tickets*, released in 2005.
3. Such as selecting aperture, filter, and other camera settings.
4. The interviewer appears to refer to Kiarostami's "unfinished cinema."
5. The translator assumes that Kiarostami is referring to *Five Dedicated to Ozu* (2003).
6. Kiarostami may have referred to *Walking in the Wind*, which was originally published in a bilingual English-Farsi edition by Harvard University Press in 2002. Suhrkamp Verlag is not publishing any book of his at the time of this translation.
7. Joseph Houssni's essay "The Contingent-Generated Documentary," published in *Film International*, makes an excellent supplemental reading to *ABC Africa* and the interview originally published by *Revolver* magazine that is reprinted in this volume. Houssni's essay discusses documentary production and the related question of the truth of the medium. See additional resources for a complete citation.

Abbas Kiarostami at Bard College with *Five*, March 4, 2007

Scott MacDonald / 2007

From *The Sublimity of Document: Cinema as Diorama* (Oxford University Press, 2019). Reprinted by permission.

The following is a reprint of a 2007 interview that is part of the book's chapter on Abbas Kiarostami. All annotations within the interview below are part of the original print. No additions were made by the editor of this book.

What follows is a revision of the transcription by Ian Jones of the Bard conversation (published in the Bard College of the Moving Image in spring, 2007).

Scott MacDonald: For those who are serious about cinema, interested in the full panoply of film history, Bard College is a special place. It is that rare college that has consistently honored independent and experimental film and video. The Bard faculty produces independent film and video work; and they mentor students who make their own explorations. In a sense, Bard creates filmmakers who function off the interstate highway of commercial cinema, off the Thruway of Hollywood narrative.

One of the pervasive images in Mr. Kiarostami's work is a car driving along a road, often a narrow dirt road. And when I see that image, I think that Mr. Kiarostami is implicitly talking about filmmaking. So my first question is, do you see your films as a "country road," as compared with the "highway" of commercial cinema?

A second question: how are your films understood in Iran? And are they widely seen there? Do Iranians see you as a mainstream filmmaker or as an experimental filmmaker?

Abbas Kiarostami: I'll answer the second question first, because I'm not sure I understand the first question. [*Audience laughter*]

It's very hard for us, as filmmakers, to know what exactly our films are. It's up to the viewers to tell us. And when you talk about "commercial," you need to define what "commercial" includes. All my films are independent, experimental. They're also "commercial" because they pay for themselves. I don't ask for money from anybody, and each film that I've made has paid for itself.

Actually, I'm surprised to know that so many of you have seen my films! When I saw *Five* [2004] in here today, it took me back. Of course, *Five* is not an easy film—it can seem too simple and its simplicity can make it difficult to understand. But the fact that you've seen *Five* and my other films makes me want to throw my hat in the air.

I do want to answer Scott's important question. As he's said, it's not a highway we're traveling in my films; it's often a very small, narrow road. But at the same time, we're also aware of the highway. We don't ignore the highway. It's very hard to be independent and experimental and totally forget about the highway. The highway gives us the opportunity to know where we are: we look at the highway so that we don't get lost.

Scott also asked whether people in Iran see my movies. Iran is the same as everywhere else. You don't know with any prevision who the viewers are. I can't tell you whether the intellectual class sees my movies, or others. I have two best friends: one is a philosopher; the other, an architect. They don't like my movies. [*Audience laughter*] However, I've met people who are illiterate, but see my movies and understand them completely. So it's very hard to tell which categories or classes of people see my movies, or understand and enjoy them.

When we distribute our films, they're not complete. Only when you, the audience, see *Five*, can it be, with your help, with your imagination, complete. Of course, sometimes you cannot relate to a film, while at other times you get into films totally. I've been so engaged by some films that I've forgotten where I was. But then, after viewing those films, I've not remembered anything about them. For me, those films are complete as soon as I've finished watching them. I've also seen movies that I didn't enjoy, during which I was always looking at my watch, thinking, "When is this going to be over?" I might even have taken a nap during the screening. But then, the next morning, when I wake up, the movie is making me think about it, sometimes for a day, or two days, or longer. I'm very interested in that kind of movie. Because this is a long-lasting movie rather than something you watch and forget. This doesn't mean that I'm against entertainment in films. But what's important for me is that after you're entertained, something about the film should remain with you.

SM: There are many fascinating dimensions to your films. We meet wonderful people in them. But I think something that strikes many American viewers, and perhaps viewers everywhere, is your interest in landscape. Your depictions of Iranian landscape are often gorgeous. I'm conscious of this, here at Bard, because Bard's own Peter Hutton is one of the great American landscape filmmakers—and the idea of looking carefully at landscape has become a tradition in American independent film.

Your early films seem more interested in urban life, but recently your films have been increasingly involved with landscape, and, in particular, with areas that seem far from urban life. Could you talk a bit about what landscape means to you and how your interest in it has evolved?

AK: An important point for all the movies I've made recently is the effect of the Iranian Revolution on filmmaking. For a time after the revolution, I thought that I'd lost my profession. And this was true for other filmmakers too. As you know, one of the first things that happened during and after the revolution is that the new people in power set fire to movies. We thought that filmmaking as a profession was finished in Iran. At that point, I started to work with photography, photography and nature. I don't know the reason why exactly. Have you seen my *Roads of Kiarostami* [2004]?

SM: I have.

AK: If you watch that movie, you don't need me to explain why I've moved toward landscape.

When, really for the first time, I began to experience landscape and nature, I enjoyed it very much; it felt good to me. I decided to make movies about nature—or at least to take my stories into the landscape. I gave the landscape to myself as a kind of reward: I told myself, "If you're a good person, I'll reward you; I'll take you into the landscape and you can make a movie there." Since then, most of my movies are about landscape. In fact, I am addicted to the landscape and nature.

As I was coming into this area today [Bard College is in Annandale-on-Hudson in the heart of the Hudson Valley], the landscape was so beautiful that I told my friend Maryan Horri who was with me that I should come here for a week and make a film about this landscape with Peter Hutton [*audience laughter, applause*]. Because it looks like he too is one with nature, with the landscape.

SM: The subtitle of *Five* is Five Long Takes. I wonder whether in fact these are illusions of five long takes. Clearly in part five there must be more than one shot. And could you talk about the choreography of sound in part five?

AK: In the last segment of *Five*, you see the moon and the sky and the moon's reflection in the water. Naturally, it took time to understand the relationship between the frogs and the moon, something I had noticed. When the moon disappeared under a cloud, the frogs would start screaming and crying. In the film it takes seventeen minutes to make that clear.

I focused my camera on the water, where the moon's reflection was moving, and in less than three minutes, the moon had disappeared—too quickly to understand the relationship between what you see and what you hear. I had to find a way to make this section longer so you could have the experience I was trying to replicate. It took me many different visits to that spot to film the moon disappearing, so that I would have enough material to create the segment.

[*Kiarostami is handed a laser pointer and points to the Caspian Sea on the map of Iran*] This is where *Five* was shot, right here. From Tehran to that spot is four hundred kilometers. Every time I went there, either the moon was visible or it was behind the clouds or sometimes I was lucky and could film it disappearing behind the clouds.

Each month I had only two nights when I could film—because I needed a full moon. And each time I had only two hours to shoot, because the moon had to be seen at a precise angle. It took me six months of traveling from Tehran to that spot, to have enough footage for that segment of *Five*.

So you're correct in assuming that the fifth segment was not one continuous take, but for most viewers, it's the same as one. In fact, it's very hard to tell that there are five or six shots. As filmmakers, sometimes we lie to you. [*Audience laughter*] If you didn't catch that lie, I'd be happy. But the experts, the critics, can detect our lies. Sometimes we have to lie; we don't have any option. But it is important to me that you to see the fifth section as one a continuous event, rather than as different shots.

SM: What was involved in doing the sound?

AK: We worked very hard on that sound. For two or three months, we just listened to the sounds of frogs and the other sounds, so that we could coordinate those sounds with the imagery in the fifth segment.

To create this kind of movie you have to love slow, careful work. You have to love the process.

SM: At the end of *Taste of Cherry*, you move from 35 mm into digital. The film ends with a digital segment. And *Five* is also a digital film. Would you have made *Five* in 35 mm if that had been financially possible? Or did you want to explore digital filming in particular?

AK: *Five* would have been impossible without digital. To shoot in 35 mm would have cost a lot of money, and nobody would have invested money in that kind of movie. The only expense I had was for the gasoline in my car. We're lucky to have the benefit of digital, because a lot of things can now be done at low cost, sometimes at no cost. You can create what you personally like.

The digital part at the end of *Taste of Cherry* was not what I wanted. The last part of the film had been destroyed, and in the end I had no choice but to use digital for the conclusion. Then I realized that this was actually a good thing. I think that it gives credibility to *Taste of Cherry*. Though it was not part of my idea for the film, that digital material was like a documentary of the life surrounding the making of the film.

Renoir once said, "When you're painting, and a drop of water falls on your painting, don't be disappointed. Do something with it; create something with it." That's actually what happened in a *Taste of Cherry*. From a problem, I created something strong. This has happened in other films. Something happens that you don't think is good, but when you look at it later, you realize that it was a blessing. Not only for the movie, but for life itself.

Audience: In *Taste of Cherry*, does Mr. Badii die?

AK: He didn't die in the movie. Or after the movie: he's still alive. Before *Taste of Cherry*, he was an architect. He quit architecture and has continued to act in movies.

SM: Most of us here know very little about Iran. And when I look at the map of Iran, I try to imagine where your films are shot. We have a map here, and I'd be very grateful if you could point out some of the locations you've used.

AK: Let me say that when I walked into this room and saw the Iranian map projected up there on the screen, I thought, "What a beautiful way of welcoming me to this building!"

I know that the picture you have of Iran from the mass media, from American television, is not really what Iran is. Can you see the beautiful shape of Iran? It's just like a sleeping cat. The Caspian Sea is above the cat, just to the side of its head, and the Persian Gulf is below. There are only four letters in "Iran"; the first day that kids go to school, they learn how to write the name of their country.

There are a lot of things that I'd like to talk about, but I'll make this short: [*Pointing to Tehran on the map*] That's Tehran, where I live. [*Points to a spot in the far north-west of Iran*] *Life and Nothing More* [1992] and *Through the Olive Trees* [1994] were produced in that area—and those films are about those areas. [*He also points to Iraq*] You know where this place is! [*Audience laughter, then Kiarostami points to Afghanistan*]. And you know that this is Afghanistan.

A few years ago, they showed one of my movies to schoolchildren in southern France. The person who was responsible for showing my movie asked the children, "Do you know where Iran is?" And only one boy raised his hand and said he knew, but it turned out that even he was mistaken. So nobody in that class knew where Iran was. This was just after the Iranian Revolution so you'd expect the world to be aware of Iran. The person who was in charge of that event told the children, "If you find or draw a map of Iran and bring it to class, you can come and watch another movie for free."

This is all by way of saying that if you paid to come here to Bard today and watch *Five* and listen to me, then I'll ask Scott to give you your money back, because you already have a map. [*Audience laughter*]

SM: One last question, before I turn this over to the audience: In 2003 you were scheduled to premiere *Ten* at the New York Film Festival, and, in what felt to me like one of the most embarrassing moments of a fairly long embarrassing period in American history, you were not able to get a visa to come to that premiere. I'm wondering if you could tell us about that incident?

AK: It wasn't really that important.

Since 9/11, it's been very difficult to get a visa to come to the United States. Before 9/11, when I'd go to the American office in Paris to get a visa, they'd give me a cup of coffee. I'd sit there for a few minutes and soon they'd hand me the visa. Since 9/11, when you go there, you don't get a cup of coffee, and they tell you to come back in two to three months. Obviously, by then, the New York Film Festival was over. So that's why I didn't come.

For my trip this week, I wanted to bring you books of my photography and my poetry, but I couldn't bring them because there's no longer a cultural relationship between our two countries.

I understand it. An event as big as 9/11 affects things in the world, and all this is part of that.

But I should also point out that before 9/11 and after 9/11, my relationships with my American friends are just the same. There has been no problem at all.

SM: Mr. Kiarostami, you're very generous. It's certainly true that we would expect that things might be different after 9/11, but to have you, of all filmmakers, not get a visa to come here is an embarrassment at any time.

AK: The reason I say it is not so important is that other things are far more important than my appearing at a film festival. I have an Iranian friend who lives in the United States. His parents wanted to come and see him, but they couldn't get a visa. Two years ago, they died without seeing their son.

And the events going on in Iraq are so enormous that sometimes I feel embarrassed to say that I live close to Iraq. I wonder who is going to take responsibility for the tragedy going on there? And the tragedies going on all over the world. If you lived twenty years ago, things were much better than what we see now.

After the revolution in Iran, the solution for a filmmaker like me was to go to a rural area, into the landscape—as a way to keep fresh. That was how I came to make *Five*.

Audience: A question about *Taste of Cherry*. I found it very interesting that the people who Mr. Badii interacts with are very different: one is a soldier from Kurdistan; I think the seminary student is from Afghanistan, and of course, that wonderful character at the end, the wise old man, is Turkish. By including this kind of cosmopolitan exchange, were you trying to say something specific for an Iranian audience that maybe we wouldn't understand?

AK: When you walk along a sidewalk in Tehran, you see Turks and Kurds and Arabs and so forth. It's just like a sidewalk in New York, where you see all different kinds of people as you're wondering where the Americans are. [*Audience laughter*]

Right now there are a lot of people from Afghanistan and from Iraq in Iran. During the time I was making *Taste of Cherry*, I'd meet people and ask about their ethnicity. Nearly all of them were Kurds or Turks or Arabs. Tehran is cosmopolitan, like New York.

Audience: How did you select the actors you would interview, and did you have to rehearse them? I mean, they scarcely do anything, but by watching their faces, we see so much. How did you achieve that?

AK: My movie *10 on Ten* [2003] responds exactly to your question.

In brief, I find the actors in my films on the street. When I begin to think about characters, I don't have a fixed idea of what I'm looking for—only a general idea. If I were to sit down and design a perfect character, it would be very hard to find that character in the real world. So I look for somebody who seems similar to the actor I'm imagining. Once I've found this person, it doesn't make any difference what he/she looks like or what language he/she speaks. I adjust my ideas about the character with respect to that person, rather than imposing my preconceived ideas for a character on the person. It's very dangerous to have a "dream" character—better to focus on the person you find.

Audience: Following up on that, I've always been interested in the way cinema is described as being "realist" or "neorealist." There's a history of "realisms" in cinema. But when you go back and look at Antonioni's "realism," as opposed to Rossellini's "realism," they turn out to be very different.

What are your ideas about realism?

AK: Rossellini, Pasolini—they're coming from the golden age of neorealist cinema in Italy, but that doesn't mean that they have the same view of "realism."

I believe that "realism" does not exist without the audience, without viewers. Consequently, "realism" changes with the viewers that we attract. When you have an idea of the real, then look through the camera, the idea of reality that you had before escapes from you. It's very hard to record "reality." When you pick a scene and choose your camera angle, your preconceived "reality" no longer exists.

This is not only in filmmaking. When you look at a couple who have been living with each other for thirty years, they see each other differently than you see them. Only a partner can understand what is inside the other partner at a given moment. That person may seem to be a certain type to you, but that person looks different to a spouse.

Audience: This is not a question, but a reflection on my reaction to *Five*. I both enjoyed being asked to work hard during that film, and I also resented it. Sometimes I felt like a conservative member of the public at the first performance of *Le sacre du printemps* [*The Rite of Spring*], and at other times I was swimming in the luxury of having gotten so much out of what I saw. All in all, it was a wonderful experience.

AK: Thank you very much for the fact that you liked my film and had something good to say about it.

Peter Hutton: About your film *Where Is the Friend's House?* [1987], which is extraordinary in its simplicity and beauty: is it, perchance, autobiographical?

AK: There are two or three stories combined. The basis for one of them is my son. Sometimes, when we relate to a segment of a movie, we can tell that there is some reality in there, that this is not just a story.

PH: I was thinking specifically about the scene where the teacher opens the book at the end and finds the flower.

AK: That moment has had an impact on a lot of people. The first effect was on me. I remember, from twenty years ago, that when I was working on that scenario, I had pain in my hand, so one of my friends was with me to take my dictation. He was a good friend, but he wrote very slowly. When we got to the end of the story, I imagined the teacher turning the page of the boy's notebook and suddenly I imagined seeing the flower that the old man had given Ahmad the night before. I got emotional and said to my friend: "Quick! Write this down!"

I didn't have that moment in mind until we got to the last page of the scenario. Once I saw that flower, there was a smile on my face and it didn't go away for a long time.

It was very important for me to see that that flower has had an effect on people all over the world. But I don't want you to think that I'm bragging about my film. [*Audience laughter*] Because this moment is not something that I created; it just happened as we worked. Sometimes things happen beyond our imagination.

SM: At what point in your life did you realize you wanted to be an artist, and specifically a filmmaker? As a child growing up, were you a moviegoer, and, if so, what films do you remember seeing?

AK: When I was young, we lived outside of Tehran, in a place that didn't have a movie theater. I was ten years old, but hadn't seen any movies. Then a movie theater opened in our area. My sister, who was four years older than me, went with me to see a film, and I remember very well the first image that I saw on the screen—because it scared me so much that I grabbed my sister's hand. It was the Metro-Goldwyn-Mayer lion!

I also remember that in the middle of that film, there was a guy with a big nose, who was playing the piano with his nose. I fell asleep before the movie ended.

Our generation—we were all interested in film, though I could not have imagined that one day I'd become a filmmaker. My friends from childhood are architects and physicians.

Audience: One quick comment, and then a question. I want to add to Mr. Hutton's appreciation of the ending of *Where Is the Friend's House?* the ending of *Close-Up* [1990]—two of the most beautiful endings in all of film.

AK: Thank you very much. Before I came here I was coughing a lot, and you've made me feel much better. [*Audience laughter*]

Audience: My question is about scriptwriting. How do you write a script for an experimental film, like the film we saw today, as opposed to a narrative film?

AK: As you know, writing a script is a long process, and I would need a whole workshop to explain the process. But, in brief: I don't write my scripts in detail; I don't decide precisely what I want to do before I find the main character that I'm interested in. I have an idea, a general idea, and then I find my characters, and I change my ideas according to what I learn about my actors and the characters they play. So the process is in between feature narrative film and documentary film.

Audience: I saw a documentary about Iranian filmmakers who had to leave Iran. It made me curious about why you've been able to stay and what sort of film community is there now. Do you communicate with ex-patriot Iranian filmmakers living in exile?

AK: After the revolution, some filmmakers left, some stayed. Those who stayed gradually tried to understand and tolerate the situation. Most of us felt we were out of a job. We weren't doing anything. Some people went into business; others, like me, turned to still photography. But eventually some of us found a way to make our films. When we started again to make films, we struggled with how we could deal with so many limitations and regulations. But we had no choice: if we wanted to make films we had to find a way.

Unfortunately, although they were good filmmakers, some of those who left Iran did not feel the need to experiment like we did: they were waiting for the time when they could go back to Iran and resume the kinds of filmmaking they were familiar with. This waiting took much longer than they anticipated, and if you wait for the kind of Iran that you want to go back to before you're willing make a film, you tend to lose your creativity. This is not to say that all of expatriate Iranian filmmakers are like this, but some of them are.

In brief, the Iranian government helps the kinds of films that it likes, mostly kinds of film that are Hollywood style, with the Islamic limitations: let's call it "Islamic Hollywood style." [*Audience laughter*]

The government has nothing to do with my movies. They neither support me nor bother me. A lot of the movies that I make don't get shown in Iran. As you know, my movies are not political, but the government doesn't support them because they don't think that these are good movies—meaning they're not the kinds of movies that most people want to go and see. So, on behalf of the people, they decide not to support my movies. [*Audience laughter*]

Audience: How will your poetics change if Iran gets attacked?

AK: By the United States, you mean? That might destroy everything, poetic and not poetic. When we had eight years of war between Iraq and Iran, it was disastrous.

But when something happens, you deal as best you can with the situation.

Audience: I'm thinking of what you said earlier about the image of Iran in American mass media. When I saw *Ten* [2002], every mass media image of Iran I had was destroyed in the first minute. For the first time I understood something of what Iran is, not what we were supposed to imagine it to be. Thank you for that.

The question I have is not political. As someone who has worked with celluloid film for a long time, what are your conclusions at this point about how the roles of the director, the cameraperson, and the editor have changed because of the emergence of digital shooting?

AK: Digital has changed a lot of things. It's like a toddler walking: we don't know where this child will go. But I believe that it will lead to new kinds of creativity in moviemaking. It may also reveal some weaknesses in those who want to make movies, but who don't find a way to be creative in the new medium.

SM: Mr. Kiarostami has been very patient, especially for a man with a bad cold, so we'll take just two more questions, and then he'll be here for a bit afterward.

Audience: A follow-up question about digital versus film. Besides the economic savings of using digital and the fact that digital might affect how much you might be willing to experiment, how do you feel about the aesthetic, perceptual differences between film and digital. Does shooting digital affect what you might want to shoot?

AK: An excellent question. A brief answer: when we use a digital camera, we have to think in a digital way. The two kinds of shooting give you two different possibilities. It's impossible to deal with some subjects without digital. For example, *Five* was only possible with digital.

Even in a movie like *Ten*, the action between the mother and her child would be very difficult to shoot without digital. Digital allowed me to stay away from the action, and let mom and her child interact with each other. When you're shooting nondigital, at least in 35 mm, a lot of people are involved—there's no privacy in celluloid shooting. And everything costs money.

There are other cases we could cite where you should only use digital if it's impossible to use a 35 mm camera, since the image quality of 35 mm is superior.

At this point it's a bit like the difference between painting with oils and working in watercolor.

SM: Last question.

Audience: I think we need to include among the great, ravishing endings in film the end of *The Wind Will Carry Us* [1999]. You seem to have a poet's intuition and belief in the image itself. But I was wondering how the end of that film came about.

AK: I'd like to thank you very much, instead of answering your question. Because at the moment, I'm sorry to say, I don't remember the ending! [*Audience laughter and applause*]

Shirin as Described by Kiarostami

Khatereh Khodaei / 2009

From *Offscreen*, vol. 13, no. 1, January 2009. Reprinted by permission of *Offscreen* and Khatereh Khodaei.

It may be an odd experience to sit in a dark movie theater, stare at the screen and see fellow audience members watching a motion picture. Personally, I believe the experience of watching a movie in which the sound of the story that we hear is different from the pictures that we watch can be more interesting.

Shirin is the latest feature film by Iranian auteur Abbas Kiarostami. It features simple close-ups of the faces of 113 actresses who are watching a movie.

After watching the film and talking with Mr. Kiarostami, I found out that the women, whose faces appeared in perpendicular frames in the film, were not actually watching a movie at all; a few fixed spots had been installed above the camera and they were acting with Kiarostami's special improvisational technique.

What makes the experience doubly interesting is to learn that the story was decided on after shooting was over. It is the love story of Khosro, Shirin, and Farhad, a masterpiece by the great Iranian poet Nezami Ganjavi. The work features effective editing and an attention to details which, as always, render Kiarostami's movies simple, different and absorbing.

Abbas Kiarostami characteristically attaches a special significance to audiences. In his latest production, *Shirin*, he goes as far as explicitly suggesting that the silver screen would be non-existent in the absence of audiences.

Shirin is the story of the empathy of audiences—the audiences who are watching the empathy of the other audiences.

Offscreen: How did it occur to you to make such a movie?

Abbas Kiarostami: It was a response to an old temptation, a very old one dating back to the days when I had become a director. It was all about watching the audiences. I believe it has its root in the fact that, in the absence of an audience, no production could be dubbed a production on its own. It is not that

I want to grease the palms of audiences. I don't seek to lift the stature of the audience at the expense of the production. What I am saying is that the moment an audience is affected by a movie, the creation is that special moment, not the film itself. There is no such thing as a movie before the projector is switched on and after the theater's lights are turned off. A film which consists of many frames that is placed in a box, or works by a digital system, etc., is nothing like a painting or statue to prompt us to think of it as a mass or an identity. I believe the identity of the silver screen hinges on audiences, in such a moment that it sees its audience. So a production takes shape in the moment we see the audience. In other words, at a certain juncture audiences and the movie become one.

I believe this work features two movies. I mean, we don't look at the production in the abstract; rather, we look at its impact on audiences. This is a very old phenomenon evident in some other films I have directed. For instance, in *Under the Olive Trees* [also known as *Through the Olive Trees*] the moment there is an argument between Ms. Shiva and Hussein with the construction worker who has dropped the bricks, we see the traffic jam without actually seeing it. I mean on their faces we see the whole atmosphere without seeing the actual congestion. It is the case in several recent productions of mine. We see the film through the impact it has on people who are watching a movie.

I had a very radical feeling and wanted to watch the audience in private. To me watching people is more interesting than anything else. This is a very old feeling. It has nothing to do with directing. It is a deep and bold gaze; similar to that of children in the cradle, quite straightforward. There are moments in this film which are just like a gift to me. It is a blessing to be able to look at someone so closely to detect feelings on their faces.

Offscreen: Where does *Shirin* stand in the list of your works, particularly as your productions are becoming more minimal?

AK: Any production is a follow-up to previous works . . . but I didn't mean to render it minimal because it is not my responsibility to summarize a production this much.

Offscreen: But that is what is happening. You once quoted a critic as saying that *Shirin* is the most radical film of Kiarostami's in its taking everything out of the frame.

AK: It is because I love simplicity. For instance, in the books I am working on right now, for example Rumi's *Diwan-e Shams*, I opt for poems which are closer to daily conversations and simple modern language. I would not opt for poems featuring very difficult words. Although some of them are great because of their rhythm, and their lyrics.

Offscreen: Now that the film is over, how do you find it when you watch it?

AK: I truly like this film very much, for a number of reasons.

First of all, the camera is fixed. Second it is "close-up" in a special sense of the word. Otherwise, I like long shots. One can see the mentality of individuals in close-ups.

Offscreen: Why did you opt for an all-female cast?

AK: Because women are more beautiful, complicated and sensational. A combination of these three qualities makes them perfect candidates for movies and for being looked at. To develop an insight into such complexity, there is no other way than watching, which is the first step on the path to research. Besides, women are more passionate. Being in love is part of their definition.

Offscreen: Tell us about the film and its script.

AK: The story was not important to me. I mean, I had not pinned my hopes on the story. I just thought they were watching a melodrama film. But I was uncertain about which film. During the course of production I came across things which I found congenial.

Nezami—who lived almost eight centuries ago—was not only able to make drama. When it came to dramatic features his works are believed to be as good as Shakespeare's; but also, he had a perfect understanding of women. The image he created of women was very positive; he portrayed women as being capable and self-reliant. Such personalities are rarely seen even today.

Although *Shirin* maintains all the feminine, intricate features of women, it proves quite strong. Nezami has created a great picture of a love triangle for us. A triangle one side of which features a king, and another an architect and mathematician, a statue maker, or an able-bodied person capable of conveying confidence to women. I believe they were both ideal for women. The story revolves around a love triangle with particular problems.

Offscreen: What reaction do you think your movie will draw?

AK: I cannot guess. "I don't care at all" is quite a cliché these days because many directors begin to use that expression after a very brief experience in filmmaking. The fact that I have never uttered that sentence over the years makes me feel comfortable saying it right now. I am not saying I don't care whether they like the film or not. What I am saying is that their not liking the movie won't affect my feelings about it. I believe I have already answered this question without answering it, by watching the film several times; whenever someone has watched the film, I have watched it too. It comes despite the fact that I have never watched my own movies, even once. Actually, *Close-Up* is an exception. I have watched it three or four times.

This film has a lot to explore. That is why when I watch it again I find something new which invites me to watch it again.

Offscreen: Do you agree that this film is ahead of its time or is very different?

AK: Yes, I believe it is very different, particularly now, a time when something is shown again and again and again; not showing is a kind of objection, an objection to that amount of showing. Pornographic films are not the only representation of porn. When an open-heart surgery is on your screen, it is pornography. Watching things which are not supposed to be watched amounts to the experience of pornography.

Maybe it is a means to object, a reaction to films which show everything. Someone who had seen the movie told me, and I quote, "when I was watching the film, I just wanted to see the things they were watching." "Do I want to see what they were watching," I asked myself? The answer was "no way, no way." I have seen those scenes again and again: horses which appear on the screen and neigh; settings which have been built on not-so-solid evidence to portray life seven thousand years ago. These decorations constantly reveal their hollow nature. I believe it is new and innovative. It features things I have never had the chance to look at from a very close distance. Whenever I miss those moments, I can watch a reconstructed TV series.

What I am seeing now is actually two films with a ticket. Because we have to think about the impact of something other than the thing itself.

Offscreen: When we hear a story, we naturally create an image in our imagination. But here there are images to look at. What do you think about the fact that in *Shirin* we do not see images related to the story we hear?

AK: Are you saying I have constrained your imagination . . . ?

Offscreen: We are in the habit of imagining what we hear, for example, a story on the radio.

AK: You mean when I am looking at someone's face, I am not as free as when I am listening to radio to let my imagination loose?

Offscreen: Exactly, and this is not what a human is used to under normal circumstances.

AK: No. This is not radio. Although you are free to imagine what you wish to, you have to see what I am showing. In fact, it is a combination of both freedom and restriction. I suggest you watch another world which is more attractive than the story. I believe if you dare let go of the story, you will come across a new thing which is the Cinema itself. In fact, I suggest you let go of the story and just keep your eyes on the screen.

Certifying the Copy: An Interview with Abbas Kiarostami

Aaron Cutler / 2010

From *Cineaste*, vol. 36, no. 2, Spring 2011, pp. 12–15. Interview conducted October 2010. Reprinted by permission.

The Iranian poet and painter Abbas Kiarostami turned to filmmaking in 1970 with a series of educational short films for children. These led to 1974's *The Traveler*, an eighty-minute work about a young boy who takes a bus ride to Tehran in order to catch a soccer game, but who falls asleep and misses the match. The film contained many of Kiarostami's eventual signatures—nonprofessional actors (with a special emphasis on children), a willingness to observe conversation, plot emerging from character, a focus on the individual's relationship to his community, and an eagerness to stop the narrative from time to time in order to look at the surrounding world.

It made sense in hindsight that he would use children so frequently in his movies, since they prove such willing witnesses. A child's journey became the subject thirteen years later of his feature *Where Is the Friend's House?*, the film that brought him international attention. The movie followed a young boy walking many miles to return a notebook to his friend in another village. The film possesses an odd, delicate melancholy that gives the viewer a sense of a person calmly taking in his environment, and discovering life and death along the way.

The person was ostensibly the film's protagonist, but it was equally the filmmaker, who in a series of subsequent masterworks found ways to feature himself within the narrative. In *Close-Up*, his most famous work, he filmed himself filming another man pretending to be a filmmaker. Sometimes, as in *Life, and Nothing More* [also known as *And Life Goes On*] and *Through the Olive Trees*, a filmmaker character visited a village to observe the inhabitants; at other times, as in *Taste of Cherry* and *The Wind Will Carry Us*, Kiarostami himself stepped into his characters' conversations, holding the camera as the other person spoke.

With their intensely first-person view, the films all but dissolved the line between truth and fiction. When asked in 1989's *Homework* what kind of work he's doing, Kiarostami replies, "It's a documentary, I guess. You can't tell until the film's made."

He went to Uganda in 2001 to film a group of orphans for the United Nations. He shot on video, intending to use the visit as research for a later return with an actual film crew, but liked the video footage so much that he edited it into the movie *ABC Africa*. As he shot on video more frequently and experimented more with the medium, Kiarostami's films became overtly formal: *10* featured ten conversations between a female driver and her passengers, *Five* showcased five long shots along the Caspian Sea and *Shirin* cut between myriad female spectators watching a film.

One spectator was the French actress Juliette Binoche, who also stars in Kiarostami's latest feature, *Certified Copy*. Binoche plays an unnamed woman (the credits call her She) living with her son in Italy, and seemingly very taken with James Miller (William Shimell), a prominent British art critic who has arrived to promote his new book. For reasons never fully explained, he visits her in her shop and they leave to spend the day together. Their conversation shifts from gettingto-know-you banter to arguments over whether he has ignored her and their child. The nature of their relationship gradually turns ambiguous, as the film leaves open whether they're playing make-believe or in fact have been married for fifteen years.

The answer, perhaps, is both. As with many of Kiarostami's previous films, it's more helpful to think of *Certified Copy* as welcoming possibilities rather than excluding them. This includes welcoming all the links that it shares with his previous works. While viewers might initially be startled by the tale unfolding in Tuscany rather than in Tehran, they might also eventually see the film more broadly as a comedy about middle- to upper-class foreigners interacting with middle- to lower-class locals, and having their assumptions about themselves challenged in the process. While it might initially feel strange to watch the luminous Binoche descend amidst a crowd of unknowns, the result is the same as in some of the director's previous films, where he deliberately placed professional actors opposite nonprofessionals to generate tension.

The film is very much a genre synthesis, the meeting place of screwball comedies of remarriage (as both Richard Porton and Miriam Bale have argued, respectively, in the *Summer 2010 Cinema Scope* and in *The L Magazine* last October) and of mid-movement Italian neorealism. But it is also very much a Kiarostami film, which, like his other great films, folds different views of reality into one greater perception. The critic's book, which shares its title with this film, argues that a copy certifies the value of its original, but the irony of his position, which she raises, is that a copy ends up taking on its own original value. The discussion spreads throughout the film to encompass more than fine art. When the couple rides in a car with the city reflected in their windshield, the reflected images take on a separate-but-equal beauty to their originals, and in turn the filmed images take on a beauty equal to the world outside the cinema. The two people walking through the city, trying out different scenarios for themselves, are multiple different copies of what a couple could be, while also their own unique selves. Binoche here becomes the director's surrogate, not just because she is the one dictating the nature of the relationship at any moment, but also because she is the professional interacting with an amateur. Shimell, an opera singer with no previous film experience, follows her like a child following an adult, and in watching them the viewer watches him learn how to play his part in the movie.

But Shimell, too, is the director's surrogate, in a largely unexplored way that marks the film itself as a copy. Credit goes to Jonathan Rosenbaum ("Watching Kiarostami Films at Home," published January 1 on jonathanrosenbaum.com) for identifying *Certified Copy* as a remake of Kiarostami's 1977 film *The Report*, also about a feuding couple, made while the director's own marriage was dissolving. In a microscopic way, *Certified Copy* reproduces myriad moments from *The Report*—for instance, *The Report*'s scene of a supervisor talking loudly on a telephone in front of colleagues mirrors *Certified Copy*'s scene of a man whipping out a cell phone during a lecture, with similar points being made about the irony of how communication devices allow people to forget each other. But in a macroscopic way, the bespectacled, hunched tax collector of *The Report* is a younger version of *Certified Copy*'s confident critic. In both films, the relationship breaks because the man works too much, ignoring his wife and child. "Work is all you do, day and night," the man's wife (a young Shohreh Aghdashloo) complains in *The Report*, foreshadowing the moment in *Certified Copy* when She bitterly bemoans how men throw themselves into work.

Both films seem to offer a cautionary tale, with work operating like a telephone—if you wish, you can wield it to block out the rest of the world. Yet if the men's conflicts converge, their decisions differ. Both films feature a shot of the man regarding himself in a mirror. In *The Report* the moment comes less than midway through the film, well before he walks out on his family. In *Certified Copy*, by contrast, the shot comes at the end of the film, and leaves open what the man does after exiting it. After many years apart, she's found him, and what he will do now that she has is ultimately left to the viewer. The film ends, literally, with a frame, welcoming both him and the spectator to the world outside the theater.

The following interview with Kiarostami was conducted at the 2010 Abu Dhabi Film Festival, where the director proved alternately candid and deliciously cryptic. Thanks to Dama Khazeni for translating Kiarostami's answers.

—Aaron Cutler

Cineaste: Your film debates whether a copy is an original work of art. How do you feel a copy is an original work?

Abbas Kiarostami: A copy is not the same thing as an original. It doesn't have the same value. But this is not to say that we estimate the copy as valueless. What I am trying to say is that it is not without any value. The value of copies is that they can direct us towards the original. I was recently at the Louvre Museum and I was filming people who were viewing the Mona Lisa. I noticed the number of ordinary people, astonished, mouths agape, standing still for long stretches looking at the work, and I wondered, "Where does this come from? Are these people all art connoisseurs?" They are like me; through the years, we've seen this work in our schoolbooks or art history books, but when we stand before the original, we hold our breath. With regards to the film there's a double meaning, which is, if you do find a good copy, grab it and stick with it and don't go after the original because you won't find it. Hence we must also think about our own possibilities. Of course, it is an ideal to have an original, but as the bartender in the film says, "L'ideale non esiste."

Cineaste: The ideal doesn't exist. The original doesn't exist.

AK: No, it does exist. We cannot say it doesn't exist. It depends a lot on your gaze. You give it that value. Nietzsche also says, "Strive so the importance is in your gaze."

Cineaste: So, for example, with those viewers before the Mona Lisa, what may be most important is that they believe they're viewing the original. Is that right?

AK: Yes. But it was behind three bulletproof sets of glass panes, and one saw it from a six-meter distance. Something like fifty thousand people view it daily. What the film is saying overall is not fundamentally about the history of art. Rather it is saying that the notion of owning an original is a notion that can harm your life. Ordinarily, all couples, all people, are looking for an original, for something exceptional. In the film, too, you encounter this because, as is said, "In my opinion it's your brother-in-law who is an original despite his lisp, because your sister looks at him as an original." There's a poem by Rumi that says:

> If you look at a div [a horned Iranian mythic monster] with grace in your gaze,
> You can see it as an angel.

Hence everything goes back to our gaze. Everything goes back to you and to the way you look. This is what the film is trying to say.

Cineaste: I sensed a relationship of the tension between a copy and an original in art to that in human relationships. There's a way in which the film's couple is simultaneously a couple that's been married for fifteen years and a couple that's meeting for the first time. Do you mean to say with this film that the way people approach a relationship dictates what it will be?

AK: Exactly. There's responsibility in a relationship, something whereby they say, "Love is the consequence of a misunderstanding." At first, when you set eyes on it, even if it's a valueless copy, you want to see it as an original. But then you take it back. Day by day, you take away points from the score, and you add negative points. That's why the relationship is destroyed. There is no care taken with the relationship.

Cineaste: Of the film's two protagonists, the Juliette Binoche character seems to be the more active creator. In what ways do you view her as an artist creating a work of art?

AK: I think we must look at her necessity, her essentiality, of the way in which she is necessary. She is the more active and the man is the more passive. In my opinion the man looks at the relationship in a more bitter fashion and the woman still holds great hopes. Therefore, in the course of the day, in the course of the encounter, it is she who leads the relationship, and the man attempts to follow.

The way you look at me reminds me a great deal of doctors. The way they listen to you describe your pain to learn whether you have a stomachache or a heartache.

Cineaste: Well, you seem in excellent health.

AK: Yes, just like that. Now you have no problems. Here is a simple prescription. If you feel fine, OK, it's not necessary to come back. Otherwise call me. But everything is fine, don't worry.

Cineaste: *Certified Copy* has quite a lot to do with your earlier film, *The Report* [*Gozaresh*], which is also about a couple. Do you see a link between the two films? If so, how have your views of couples changed since?

AK: I have to confirm that's the case. I believe that insight is accurate. It's a question no one had asked me till now, and till now I had not thought about it. Now I'm thinking perhaps this is the same man from *The Report*, who's older now, and I am the same man who made that film, only older now. Could be. I don't generally derive my stories from novels. I try to turn into film things I have felt or experienced.

Cineaste: If the man in *Certified Copy* is the same as in *The Report*, is She also the same woman? If so, how has she changed?

AK: They could be the same people, the same man and the same woman, but unfortunately we usually do not change a lot.

Cineaste: How is that same man different from thirty-five years ago?

AK: That's such a good question. Honestly, I would have to put these films next to each other and think. It seems to me that in that earlier period this man was more pessimistic, more hopeless. I think he had no desire to continue living, as I recall some of those scenes. He's completely bitter and passive, but in the new film he has some capabilities for governing his life. He might not be happy living alone, but he believes it's one solution. He thinks, given his new awareness about his situation and about the woman, in another way he can give meaning to life. In the earlier film he was only hopeless, unable to find a reason to continue living, but the man in the course of *Certified Copy*, I think, has found meaning.

It's exactly like I said, see? Little by little you're turning into a psychologist with these questions. You're forcing me to think a little. You know, I really haven't seen *The Report* in a long time. I don't have a copy, but I'll have to see it again. I think it would be good to put both these men next to each other.

Cineaste: You mentioned psychology in comparing the character and the filmmaker. To what extent were you speaking about yourself in the answer you just gave?

AK: I have answered this indirectly, but if you'd like me to answer it directly, I can. My indirect answer was, anything I've not experienced I do not look to for a subject. I have to feel it.

But the man is not at all negative. He does not have a negative character. He gives the woman small opportunities to take him wherever she wants, and this is perhaps in order to gain more of an understanding, because he wouldn't mind learning a little more about himself, about his own position and situation. The moment, in the last shot, where he looks in the mirror, I could consider the answer to all these questions. It's very indeterminate. He's received an offer. It's not definitive whether he is going to be able to decide to stay or to go. That's why I say it's not hopeless. Because at this point, when a new figure of thought occurs to him, he doesn't resist it. At the end of the film, when he's close to the camera, I think he was calculating all of these things. The machine of his mind was continually working, as if he was looking at himself.

Cineaste: You're talking about this man learning to take control of his destiny. The man's activation of his own destiny has something to do with the relation between cinema and the outside world. You have a contrast between the two performers, this actor who is an actor, but who has never acted in film before, versus an actress who has an enormous amount of performance experience and is immensely aware of herself as a screen performer. Was this contrast important to you?

AK: Yes. I think the contrast between these two in the professional world of cinema mattered to me. One who has reached the ultimate point of being a star, who knows how to do everything very well, facing another person who would throughout the making of the film transfer his anxiety to both of us, to me and to Juliette, as to whether or not he would be capable of fulfilling his role. This in itself created a challenge that was actually very good for me, since I hadn't ever counterposed two such performers before, creating that challenge between someone who knows their part and someone who doesn't. This is not something that a spectator understands about the film, that one knows and the other doesn't know how to act. But this in itself, I think, transmitted a sense of anxiety to both of them that helped the idea that they are a couple and not actors. This anxiety between them produced two kinds of estrangement that were very good for the film.

Cineaste: In your film *On Five* [also known as *Five*], you referred to your project at that time [2003] as "one-word cinema." For the past decade, you've been making works that can safely be called minimal. What led you from making one-word cinema to a film with as rich a vocabulary as *Certified Copy*?

AK: The one-word cinema wasn't possible for me anymore. I'd hit a wall, a dead end. Therefore I thought I'd turn back. There's a poem that says:

> Unsure, I stand at the crossroads
> The only way I know is the way back.

Kiarostami's View into Iran's Future

ORF.at / 2011

From ORF.at, February 11, 2011. © ORF.at. Reprinted by permission. Translated by Monika Raesch. Dalibor Manjic, ORF.at, led the conversation.

The situation for filmmakers in Iran is volatile—not just since the arrest of director Dschafar Panahi. In an interview with ORF.at, Panahi's internationally renowned colleague Abbas Kiarostami explains why auteur filmmakers cannot be silenced in his home country.

ORF.at: Iranian auteur cinema is increasingly a topic in the media. What is the situation for filmmakers in Iran in general, and how is the situation for the new generation of independent filmmakers in Iran in particular?

Abbas Kiarostami: It is difficult to receive shooting permits and financial grants, as the government only wants to support and screen one type of film: films that entertain. Auteur cinema is not supported. The new generation of filmmakers does not get distracted by that though. They don't need permits or [financial] support from the state, as they shoot with their own new equipment, such as digital cameras. With this approach—pretty much unbelievable—around one thousand short and documentary films have been made annually in Iran. Most are very good—in any case, better than commercial films.

ORF.at: Are filmmakers in Iran discouraged when they follow the case of Dschafar Panahi, including the verdict? [ORF.at: prosecuted by the Revolutionary Court and sentenced to six years on probation.] And how could the Cause Panahi develop?

AK: I believe in a turnaround in the case of Dschafar Panahi. Things can't continue like this, not in the long term. Many, many people all over the world are shocked and upset about the verdict [and sentencing]. Especially filmmakers—inside Iran and outside of Iran—are currently putting pressure on the government to improve the situation. It is simply unfair that a filmmaker can be threatened with six years imprisonment—one can't do that. I am confident and hope that the sentence will at least be lightened.

In regard to the younger generation of filmmakers, I believe that such action on part of the government as we have seen against Dschafar Panahi will not stop young auteur directors—simply because filmmakers love the cinema and film too much and want to be filmmakers at any cost.

ORF.at: Mohammed Rasulef, a colleague of Dschafar Panahi's, is expected to receive a twenty-year ban from performing his profession.

AK: I believe that must be a joke. No one can seriously mean that. In my whole life, I have never heard of any filmmaker in any country anywhere in the world to have received such a penalty. The only thing I can imagine is that a film is banned, like it happened to me. In Iran, my movies have not been screened in fourteen years. But that doesn't matter.

ORF.at: Which movies of yours have not been screened in Iran, that is, are not permitted to be screened?

AK: All my films since *Taste of Cherry*, *The Wind Will Carry Us*, *Ten*, also not *Five Dedicated to Ozu*, not *Tickets* and also not *10 on Ten*, and so on.

ORF.at: How do you deal with your films not being permitted to be screened?

AK: Of course, it is difficult, but what can I do? It is what it is. More or less, I can hope that people in Iran will get a chance to purchase my films on the black market and to watch them that way. Regardless, I cannot and don't want to stop working, just because my films are not screened in Iran. Okay, they don't screen my films; yet I continue to shoot new ones.

ORF.at: What does the shoot of your new film look like?

AK: Short films can be realized inside Iran without a permit. I shoot feature films outside of Iran. I can't do it any other way.

ORF.at: On February 11, a new announcement of solidarity toward Dschafar Panahi is expected to take place. Joining are international film stars including Steven Spielberg, Martin Scorsese, and Francis Ford Coppola.

AK: The situation in my country is different from every other country in the world. At least we are living through some very specific times. It is completely unclear what the future will bring. I am not a pessimist. But, unfortunately, at the moment I don't have much hope. Personally, I believe everybody will find their own way—of course, I don't know a formula for every filmmaker, as people have different personalities—to improve the situation as a whole.

ORF.at: Do the cinemas and the international filmmaker collective have the power to improve the situation in Iran?

AK: We have the power of cinema and that of films, not only the power of directors. Films can develop an unbelievable power, socially speaking. I believe that the strong international film industry reaction to Dschafar Panahi's arrest occurred because people like auteur cinema in general and support Panahi's film, and not because Dschafar Panahi is a colleague. Generally speaking, films garner lots of attention; that's our chance. A large number of intellectuals, writers, politicians, activists are imprisoned, but no one has received so much support as Dschafar Panahi. That's a response of solidarity for the cinema, for movies.

ORF.at: You have been directing films for about forty years and have been a juror multiple times at renowned film festivals. Which one was your first festival?

AK: My first film festival attendance was somewhere in the south of France; it was called "Politics Film Festival." That was in 1972, and I screened my second film of intermediate running time. I didn't have good experiences with my first and second film festivals. They were horrible. Back then, we had a similar situation in our country [Iran] as we have today; every time I visited a festival, every single journalist and even some directors asked me about Iran's political situation and didn't ask about my films. I constantly had to remind them that I am not a politician but a filmmaker.

So it was very similar back then as it is today. I didn't like it back then and still don't like it now. I took a break from film festivals for twelve years after these first two experiences. During that time, I exclusively focused on my work and directed one film after another. Only then did I decide to return to a film festival—Cannes.

ORF.at: What advice do you give directors, especially the new generation of filmmakers?

AK: I don't have any particular advice. Everyone can and will find their own way. The new generation of directors—especially if they start their careers without having many possibilities in the film world—should try to view their starting point as a chance and opportunity and to use it to find a completely new way to tell a story to establish a connection with the audience. I own a film school in Tehran and work with young filmmakers; and every year—not just in Iran but in many other countries around the world—directors have very different starting points. These should be used to find a new way to tell one's own story. In one's specific own way. My wish for the future is that there will be more new film styles. Nowadays, you have many filmmakers who copy others and whose primary goal is to make a profit with their film and to entertain the audience. When you are a beginner, a young filmmaker, who doesn't have many options but has lots of courage, then one should use that to create a new style. I hope that such movies will find a new way [in the existing film world]. In the cinema, [I want to see films] in which I can see the personality of each individual director.

A Very, Very, Very Bad Situation

Ulrike Timm and Waltraud Tschirner / 2011

From *Deutschlandfunk*, October 13, 2011. Reprinted by permission of Ulrike Timm.
Translated by Monika Raesch.

Iranian director Abbas Kiarostami shot his first film, *Certified Copy*, outside of his home country. He shot it in Italy—starring Juliette Binoche and William Shimell. The situation for directors in Iran is currently so poor that he will also shoot his next film far away from his home country of Iran, this time in Japan.

Ulrike Timm: Abbas Kiarostami is one of the great filmmakers of our time. The established Iranian master of cinema captivates with a peculiar imagery; he enjoys improvisation and prefers to work with nonprofessional actors. Now, his first film shot outside of Iran arrives in movie theaters, and it was realized completely differently: *Certified Copy* is its name. And my colleague Waltraud Tschirner had the opportunity to ask Abbas Kiarostami a few questions on the phone.

Waltraud Tschirner: Juliette Binoche—this woman is all sensuality. Even as a heterosexual woman, one cannot often turn one's gaze away from her. Did you think of casting her from the very beginning as you were planning this film?

Abbas Kiarostami: I think this is my final interview about this film, *Certified Copy*. Up until this moment, no one had described Juliette Binoche as the embodiment of sensuality. I think she would likely be happy to hear this, that she is viewed in the film as an icon of sensuality. It was not my intention to cast her for this film, but it is correct: the film's basic constellation required a woman with an erotic, sensual, well, possibly also a sexy charisma. And it is the case that she uses both those weapons—eroticism and emotion—well; if we shall call them that. She knows how to utilize them [as an actress].

WT: You are never a missionary; you are also never dogmatic. If I understand you correctly in the way I understand your films, you are more of a stimulator of thoughts. You created a beautiful place for projection with *Certified Copy*, in that every viewer can ponder their own thoughts and conditions in regard to love, relationships, and life form. We can measure ourselves [against these characters], rub up against them and work off them. Taking my perspective, did this film become an example of an ideal example for good cinema?

AK: You don't expect that I will confirm your statement, which is one full of praise for me? That is very difficult!

WT: Well, it would be my ideal scenario!

AK: Let me say something that may be an indirect answer to your question: when I completed the script, I sent it to Juliette Binoche. After she had read it, she told me that, on one hand, she had to laugh a lot, but on the other hand, she also experienced being upset. Then, she shared that her boyfriend had also read the script and she had to calm him down and assure him that she had not given any details about their private day-to-day lives to me. She explained to him that the story originated solely in my own life experience, from my own knowledge about life.

The story continues: the role of the main male character was originally to be portrayed by Robert De Niro. So I sent the script to Martin Scorsese, asking him to please forward it to De Niro. First, Scorsese read it himself; then he sent a brief note to me. He wrote: "At first, I laughed a whole lot, and by the end, I was very sad, as I saw the women of my own life in front of my inner eye as I was reading [your script]." One needs to know that Scorsese did not have a shortage of women.

WT: Well, with this anecdote, you basically ruined my next question: Robert De Niro did not end up playing the role, but William Shimell did. This [change in casting] permitted me to think: "well, Shimell is known on the opera stage, but he has done little film work." Kiarostami cast him because of that, since it is well known that he likes to work with nonprofessional actors. William Shimmel is a bit of a novice actor in this film. So was it a good casting choice to work with him, if Robert De Niro was unavailable?

AK: So, first of all I have to praise you for this truly beautiful question: yes, actually, in the end I did like that Robert De Niro [did not play the part]. Of course, I could understand Juliette's wish for a kind of male counterpart, a similarly famous actor. But it didn't work out and I was happy, just as you say. Shimell is very well known as an opera baritone, but not as a professional actor. I thought to myself that that may be precisely the reason he would be a good counterbalance to Juliette Binoche. What I didn't imagine though: he ended up being so brilliant that I asked Juliette, "And, how was it, would you have preferred De Niro by your side?"—and she answered, "No, no, he was a wonderful colleague to be working with."

WT: You have said in an interview that creativity is like being with a pregnant woman. She doesn't know whether it's going to be a boy or a girl and whether the child will look like her or like dad. And I will add now, or whether it will be twins in the end, whether identical, fraternal. Do you yourself, Abbas Kiarostami, want to always be surprised; do you want to give room for a spontaneous inspiration, and is that a reason why you are such a big supporter of improvisation?

AK: Yes, but unfortunately, by now, the movie, the cinema no longer has space for true creativity. Everything has to be finalized for a project in advance: when you start shooting, the wrap date, the budget anyway, the cast, and everything else as well. And all that happens on the basis of profit considerations. That means there is no more room for true creativity; it falls by the wayside.

WT: Do you have an idea how this situation could be changed? After all, you are trying to improvise again and again, regardless.

AK: Yes, that is absolutely possible. But with very subtle considerations and in a way that the law of cinema is not impacted. After all, it is like this: when cinema emerged, it was supposed to be an art form, the seventh art. Over time, the cinema has turned into an industry. Just look to the US, [look to] Hollywood, then you know what I mean.

It is correct that the time of script development and of production are similar to a pregnancy. And as you said, one never really knows what the end product is going to be. But by applying some subtle improvisation, a filmmaker can make it a little more bearable, in the same way one attempts to make pregnancy more comfortable [for a woman]. Of course, one cannot violate the brazen laws of filmmaking, but one can make changes under the radar so to speak with small, smart improvisations.

WT: It is well known that you don't like to be taken hostage for political interviews about your country. For instance, last year, at the festival in South Korea, you were indignant when you were asked about Jafar Panahi. But our listeners likely expect that you will comment on the current situation in Iran. So: how can one, how can you currently work as a filmmaker in Iran?

AK: First of all, I cannot leave the first part of your question without a response. So, the question I always, always, always receive about my colleague Jafar Panahi. I can answer to that. So, regarding Jafar Panahi, there was a time when he had already been released from custody, which could have been known, but I was asked about him every time.

What annoys and upsets me is the reaction by the West, the reaction by Panahi himself, and also the reason [given] by the Iranian government. It is like no one wants to verbalize that Panahi had long been released. Well, he is free; he even made a movie that was screened at Cannes, and he is already in conversations about contracts on possible future film projects.

I simply don't understand why no one says it that explicitly and openly. It annoys me that the West doesn't seem to acknowledge that he is no longer in prison. And that is why I respond annoyed. Because I am repeatedly confronted with the question, as though nothing has changed. Truly, no one is willing to acknowledge the simple truth that Panahi is no longer in custody.

So, and now I will answer your question how one can currently work as a filmmaker in Iran. Very concrete: it is a very, very, very bad situation. It's not out of the blue that I shot this film in Italy, in a language I don't understand at all. And I will shoot my next film in Japan. Why does that happen? Of course, it has to do with the extremely complicated situation for filmmakers in Iran. That's the answer. I make my movies in foreign countries, in Italy and in Japan.

WT: Iranian director Abbas Kiarostami and his new film *Certified Copy*, shot in Italy, will arrive in theaters this week.

Communication Is the Most Selfless of All Art Forms

Andreas Busche / 2011

From *taz*, October 13, 2011. Reprinted by permission. Translated by Monika Raesch.

For this interview, all notes were added by the editor of this book.

In a *taz* conversation, Abbas Kiarostami covers universal art, reading tea leaves in film, and lack of understanding between women and men.[1]

Born in Teheran in 1940, he is the most well-known and successful Iranian filmmaker. Among his films are *Where Is the Friend's House?* (1987), *Through the Olive Trees* (1994), and *Taste of Cherry*, for which he was awarded the Golden Palm at Cannes.

taz: Mr. Kiarostami, as a humanist, what drove you to regard human relationships in European art?

Abbas Kiarostami: I don't want to be tied down geographically. Art is universal; it extends across all people, just as the sky does. I could have shot the same film in China. My apologies, if you are a little bit familiar with the political situation in Iran, you may understand my answer and it wouldn't sound rude to you.

taz: No worries, I don't think your answer was rude. Let me rephrase my question in a more general way. In *Certified Copy*, you attempt to use both art and love as mirrors for one another, and you use Juliette Binoche's and William Shimell's characters as your medium. What do you take from this dialogue?

AK: To me, communication is the most selfless and richest of all art forms. If we were to—occasionally—give the same attention and effort which we give in importance and search for the "condition humaine" to art to fellow human beings, I am certain that it would be possible to experience deeper and more intense connections with other people.

taz: You just said that *Certified Copy* could take place anywhere. For a European viewer, it appears as though you were referencing a European cinema tradition.

AK: My film extends way beyond Europe. It plays in Italy, but the characters speak in a universally understood world language, that is, English. To make a direct reference to the film, who says that Da Vinci's *Mona Lisa* only belongs to Europe? I am certain that even the schoolbook of a fifth grader in China includes a photograph of Gioconda. My references in this film are rooted in a European tradition, that's correct, but they are part of a collective memory.

taz: In your new film, you are not responding to specific motives in European cinema history?

AK: I assure you, I am not a man of reaction. Art is a place of action.

taz: The meeting between William Shimell and Juliette Binoche starts off ambiguous. Watching the film a second time, small discrepancies in behavior [between the characters] become apparent, which retrospectively shine a new light on the relationship. Do you have such details in your script or is something like this created spontaneously on the set?

AK: If you watch my film several times, then it can certainly happen that you make new connections that you fill with meaning. I only shot my film once, under very controlled conditions. It's not my intention to plant clues into a film. It is absolutely valid though to read into a film similar as one reads tea leaves.

taz: But you cannot deny that you provide the audience with an unclear picture as to the relationship between the characters. You say that there are no clues that can determine the relationship between the two?

AK: The answer to your question is simple. I show two periods in a relationship in chronological order. While doing so, I omit using classical filmic storytelling tools such as flashbacks or text graphic inserts. In the first half of the film, the man and woman get to know one another; the second half takes place fifteen years later when they are already separated.

taz: With this answer, you just gave away the sweet secret of your film.

AK: There is no secret. The mystery doesn't lie in the film itself or in the interactions of the actors, but in its structure. One single title—fifteen years later—or a dissolve to suggest a jump in time, would turn the structure into an established convention. Suddenly, we would just watch a simple love story that does not raise questions. It wasn't my intention to trick the audience. Rather, I wanted to prove Robert Bresson's dictum, that we create via deduction, not via addition.[2]

taz: So, your film is an average love story?

AK: I hope that I will never shoot a conventional love story. The sense of a love story is to personally grow and have revelations in a relationship with another person. If that doesn't happen, then we are only confronted with our own failure [if the relationship ends]. I want to provide the audience with an understanding. You could say that that claim connects all my films.

taz: And what is the understanding in *Certified Copy*?

AK: That men and women will never understand each other. That is an important understanding. Isn't it also a great final thought for this interview? I know to appreciate this understanding.

Notes

1. *taz* is a Berlin-based daily newspaper, with its online home at taz.de.
2. Bresson (1901–1999) was a French filmmaker. His book *Notes on the Cinematographer*, originally published in 1975, continues to be key reading for filmmakers and theorists.

"The Ideal Me and the Real Me"

Arash T. Riahi / 2016

From *ray Filmmagazin*, November 2016. Reprinted by permission of Andreas Ungerböck and Arash T. Riahi. Translated by Monika Raesch.

For this interview, all notes were added by the editor of this book.

The Austrian Film Museum honors the late iconic Iranian filmmaker Abbas Kiarostami, who passed away in July of this year. The Austrian director and producer Arash T. Riahi, who was born in Iran, wrote a personal, crucial, and loving eulogy for *ray*.

First, I am no Kiarostami expert. I only met him once, in a hospital in Vienna—more about that later. We were not befriended, nor did we have any other connection, besides sharing Iranian heritage and me also making films. I have to clarify right away that I have been living in exile in Austria for more than thirty years. I never returned to Iran and therefore also don't have any unique insight into Iranian society. I condemn any form of nationalistic behavior. That may sound like I am indifferent to Kiarostami's work; far from it. He shaped me, and likely many other filmmakers, and brought me closer to a modern neorealist form of cinema. His work gives me hope and gifted me with impressions from Iran that I would likely have never seen, given that I am living in exile. For that, I am deeply grateful to him. Principally speaking, I do not appreciate hero worship, because the more you study the details of the respective hero's life, the more you find out about things that one shouldn't know about. A recurring motif in Kiarostami's films is the act of looking at one aspect of reality from various truths or perspectives. The more one studies his life, these varying perspectives exist about him as well.

    I watched a Kiarostami film for the first time in the nineties, during an Iranian week of film that took place in Vienna. One of its curators was the Armenian Iranian film critic Zaven Ghokassian. Back then, a deep friendship connected us that would last until his death, two years ago. It was he who wrote the first book of Kiarostami interviews in Iran, and who would always share with me the secret storyline of the respective upcoming Kiarostami film, when he visited the Viennale annually.[1] We spent many hours together in the cinema. During the Viennale, sometimes [we watched together] up to six films in a day. Once in a while we also fell asleep in the cinema, and we each hoped that the other would not sleep at the same time, so that at least one of us watched the film and could share with the other.

I watched Kiarostami's masterpiece *Nema-ye nazdik* (*Close-Up*, 1990) with Zaven; it's still my favorite Kiarostami film. This half-documentary hybrid film is about a poor man who loves the movies and who personifies his favorite filmmaker Mohsen Makhmalbaf. He deceives a rich family into believing that he will shoot a film in their house. When the lie is uncovered, the man is put in jail, where Kiarostami, who had read about him in the newspaper, visits him. Eventually, the story is being re-created with the participation of the actual man, but every person had their own perspective of what had occurred. Kiarostami once said: "What this film is about is the difference between the 'ideal me and the real me.'"

Close-Up was not scripted months in advance but was being (re)written anew daily. Kiarostami had been permitted to film the courtroom proceedings; he shot during the day and wrote during the night. Reality pushed him along, just as it would again later for *Va zendegi edameh darad* (*And Life Goes On*, 1992) and for *ABC Africa* (2001). His curiosity for his protagonist permits the latter to blossom in front of the camera, to say unexpected things that illustrate how much art, in this case the cinema, can be an anchor for people from lower socioeconomic backgrounds, when it dedicates time to their worries and problems. *Close-Up* is an unbelievably modern film: it jumps between different time periods; it changes narrator perspectives, and it is a meditation about the power of cinema. An anecdote illustrates Kiarostami's openness regarding this film: when the film was shown at the Munich Film Festival, two rolls of film were accidentally swapped by the projectionist in the middle of the film. Kiarostami did not want to stop the film in the middle of the screening and attract attention, so he continued watching the screening, and he enjoyed the film much more in this version than in its original chronological order. After having returned to Iran, he himself changed the order of the rolls, and with it, the final version of *Close-Up* was born.

Much has been said and written about Kiarostami. Even without an Academy Award, he is the most important Iranian filmmaker; his honest, seemingly realistic cinema, devoid of technical gimmicks, free of complicated mise-en-scene, even freed from its director, as Kiarostami repeatedly remarked, was welcomed universally and understood globally. Kiarostami always compared filmmaking to soccer. Even in a good soccer team, a coach puts together the good team, practices with them, explains to each member their unique role. When the game begins, the coach cannot do much more than stand on the sideline, walk up and down, be annoyed or happy. But that doesn't mean that the director is not the author and does not have attitude. What was the attitude of this director, who managed to make such tender, peaceful films living under one of the most regressive and brutal regimes in the world?

Undoubtedly, he was a humanist, who was genuinely interested in the intricacies of human behavior; critics agree on this point. At the same time, he was not a vocal critic of the Iranian regime. Possibly his behavior was more subversive, showcasing the ridiculousness of the regime of the Islamic Republic; an innocent kiss on the cheek he gave to Catherine Deneuve at the presentation of the Golden Palm in Cannes when he received the award for his dark masterpiece *Ta-me guilass (Taste of Cherry,* 1997). Initially, the outrage about his behavior was bigger in the Iranian media than the praise for winning the award. Undoubtedly, Kiarostami was a realist who didn't necessarily want to confront or create trouble in Iran, to be able to continue to produce work, and here and there he did some things [to enable him to work], sometimes deliberately but at other times likely also not deliberately. Critics don't like to write about this, as it does not fit well in the narrative of an independent, humanistic genius, whose films were prevented from leaving the country or were banned temporarily from being screened in the country. He was surprisingly direct in an interview for the magazine *Salam-Honar va Adabiat*: "Our presence on the international cultural establishment is very important to change the perception in the West that our nation and regime are terrorists."

He was aware that his films would have the most impact if he would be able to continue to shoot them in Iran. Many of his fans view his later works, those films that he had to shoot outside of the country, such as the film with Juliette Binoche,[2] as the weaker ones in his body of work. In an interview, he once remarked that he had to deal with lots of restrictions when shooting films in Iran. With the films he shot outside of Iran, while he experienced all freedoms, he couldn't seize them. For too long, his thought processes had been impacted by the restrictions he had worked under previously. In a 2005 interview, he said: "When you take a tree with its many roots away from one place and plant it elsewhere, it won't bear fruit anymore. And even if it does, then the fruit won't be of the great quality it was in the original place. Had I left my country, I would be like the tree. I genuinely believe that I produced my best work in Iran."

He did not ever experience the fate of his filmmaker colleague Amir Naderi, who was critical of the regime. Naderi became famous with his films *Aab, baad, khaak* (*Water, Wind, Dust*, 1989) and *Davande* (*The Runner*, 1990), which were later released as Kiarostami's *Khane-ye doust kojast* (*Where Is the Friend's House?*,

1987).³ Naderi went into exile in America and left Iranian culture and content behind. He tried, at first without success, to get closer to Western culture and to find other themes for his films. It took many years for him to find a new place in film history, to recenter himself and to define himself without nostalgic reflection to his lost homeland. He was honored for his life's work in Venice in 2016.⁴

Kiarostami never intentionally wanted to be confrontational and selected topics that were innocent and impossible to attack; topics that could be interpreted in many ways.⁵ That ability was part of his talent to produce art. To not experience confrontation in a dictatorship, one must play by the rules. Those rules say that even if someone appears to act nonpolitically, they still need to support the stability of the existing system. Sometimes that happens without one's own [intentional] actions. Likely, Kiarostami often became an unwanted pawn for the Islamic regime, which always took credit for his successes when it served their purpose. For instance, simultaneously with the regime not wanting to screen *Taste of Cherry* at the Cannes Film Festival, Iran was in the news for other negative press. German investigators proved in the so-called Mykonos process that the Iranian government was responsible for the murders in the Berlin restaurant.⁶ That was a big embarrassment [for Iran] and resulted in numerous countries calling back their ambassadors to Iran. It was exactly at that time that Iranian officials, including politicians who took the stand at the Mykonos process, felt that it would be advantageous to permit screening of Kiarostami's film at Cannes to create some positive propaganda to balance out the negative news. A quote by the weekly magazine *Haftenameje Film* (No. 260) clearly articulates what occurred: "The success of Kiarostami's film is a success for the Islamic regime. Iran succeeded by selecting the correct handling of its cultural/religious actors to neutralize any opponents' criticism by winning the Golden Palm. . . . Hopefully, Amir Naderi will realize what advantages our government can provide. Kiarostami would have never gotten this opportunity were it not for the Islamic government." Without carrying "guilt" himself, Kiarostami and other likeminded, talented artists enabled the reactionary system that is also an enemy to cultural production to polish its image, even though the country leads the world annually with the highest number of executions. The Japanese distributor once said, "One suggested to us that the regime is bloodthirsty, but when I saw these films, it became apparent to me that the Western view cannot be true."

Of course, Kiarostami did not conceive his work for this purpose. He was a tireless artist, who was at home in many disciplines, such as photography, videoart, also lyrics. Likely, he only wanted to be creative and to be left alone. To be able to do so, it was necessary to make unnecessary comments at times. That's the only way I can explain his 1994 comment in response to the arrest of regime-critical author Ali-Akbar Saidi Sirjani. He was asked for a response and replied: "I don't like intellectuals who don't want to accept reality." Saidi Sirjani died several months later under unclear conditions in an Iranian prison. He had criticized the system, and indeed, he did not want to accept its reality.

Likely, the most incomprehensible behavior took place during the 2005 Iranian presidential elections, when Kiarostami wrote an open, almost amorous letter to Mahmoud Ahmadinejad, in which he emphasized how much he appreciated the man and his moral principles, and that while he gave him his heart, he would vote for the other candidate, Rafsanjani, as he would be better suited for the current needs of the country. One can interpret this as a naïve emotional action or that Ahmadinejad successfully deceived him and millions of other Iranians. One could also view it as a clever play in a chess game to not end up on the wrong side, regardless of who won the election. Unfortunately, with this letter, Kiarostami lost a majority of regime-critical fans both inside and outside of Iran. Toward the end of his life, a critic asked him what he was proud of [having accomplished during his lifetime]. He answered modestly, though his answer could also be interpreted in a couple of ways: "I don't think the word proud should be used in the context of humans. I am not proud of anything." To watch Kiarostami's films means to reject preconceptions,[7] and that is the case with every decision made in the production of a film; one creates *one* reality, one selects *one* camera angle, with every cut, some material disappears forever, and so on.

Nonetheless, I believe that Kiarostami proved his humanity precisely because he diverged from his ideal I. Who of us can say how we would behave if we were living under a dictatorship? Abbas Kiarostami was a very fine human being. He was someone who was so sensitive that he avoided many problems—with the exception of Catherine Deneuve! Often, he simply engaged in his favorite activity: to take his still camera, to sit in his car, and to go for a ride. Leaving behind the big city, politics, the complexities of everyday life in Iran, and turning to nature, to the basis of all life, to childhood, to love, to the simple details, for which others don't have any time or have become blind toward. His possible weakness turned into his strength and enriched us and the cinema, creating an unforgettable, indispensable chapter that will stand the test of time. In contrast, the Iranian dictatorship will become history sooner or later.

The only time I met Kiarostami in person was two years ago at the Vienna General Hospital. My friend Zaven Ghokassian was on his deathbed, when suddenly the door opened, and Abbas Kiarostami entered the room. He had been invited to an awards ceremony and arrived together with his friend Said Manafi, another Kiarostami biographer and filmmaker, to visit his old friend one last time. Once again, the master had left the center of life behind, to focus on the simple life. Unfortunately, death is a part of the simple life.

Notes

1. The Festival Viennale is Austria's most important international film festival, taking place annually in October.
2. The author refers to *Certified Copy* (2010), which was shot in France.
3. IMDb.com lists *The Runner* as having been written and directed by Naderi in 1984, preceding *Where's the Friend's House?* (1987). It is left unclear why the author makes a direct connection between Naderi's two films and Kiarostami's work. Naderi is not listed in the credits of Kiarostami's film. Reading the plot summaries of both of Naderi's films, it can be posited that Kiarostami's *Where's the Friend's House?* shares narrative themes with the other movies.
4. Amir Naderi was honored at the 73rd Venice Film Festival with the Jaeger-LeCoultre Glory to the Filmmaker award.
5. The translation of the sentence may result in ambiguous meaning. The original sentence used some vocabulary that left meaning open to interpretation. For this reason, the original sentence is added here, for those readers with command of the German language: "Kiarostami wollte nie bewusst anecken und suchte sich Themen aus, die so unaufgreifbar und unschuldig waren, dass sie in vielfacher Weise interpretiert warden konnten."
6. In 1997, a German court convicted four men of the 1992 murders of dissident Iranian Kurdish leaders in a Berlin restaurant and implicated Iran's leaders as having ordered the killings.
7. As was the case previously in this article, the original sentence left meaning open to interpretation. For this reason, the original sentence follows for readers to form their own meaning: "Kiarostamis Filme anzusehen heißt also, unfreiwillig auch wegzuschauen, und so verhält es sich wohl auch mit jeder filmischen Entscheidung für die *eine* Realität, die *eine* Kameraeinstellung, mit jedem Schnitt, der Material für immer verschwinden lässt, usw."

Coda

For students reading this book, the following is especially for you. That said, aren't we all students of some kind? We may not be enrolled in an official degree program in higher education or attending a high school film class. But we are all students of life. Sometimes it's a formal learning experience of a particular subject; most of the time, though, we learn from real life throughout the day. For instance, we see a parent with a stroller and a little one, trying to open a door. The automatic door switch is not working and the stroller is also very wide, making it difficult to fit through the door in any case. You approach, open the door, and hold it. How does the parent react? How does that make you feel? How would you have felt had you not helped? Life is a great (informal) teacher. While Abbas Kiarostami is unfortunately no longer with us, we still have the option to immerse ourselves in his teachings, and he will be asking you to look at "ordinary life" for your next project.

Before immersing ourselves in an excerpt of one of his filmmaking workshops, let us consider the pandemic context that we have lived through and during which this book was edited. Anyone involved in academia, whether student or faculty, can likely relate to the filmmaker's example on assignment prompts. Often, students wish they had more freedom in an assignment, but when given an assignment that gives more choice, it takes more time to have an idea that a student feels is worth pursuing. Restrictions provide guidance, lead creative thoughts down a particular path. Arguably, without any path it is much harder to conceptualize something. One has to build a path first, and that takes a lot of energy and time.

During the pandemic, many schools in the US followed film industry guidelines in regards to teaching video production classes. Additionally, a student's respective place of higher education also considered risks and likely placed additional restrictions specific to the school. This meant that assignments were likely significantly different than they otherwise would have been, as was the in-class environment. Besides the obvious, which is wearing masks, face shields, and possibly also gloves, video equipment could not be shared. As a result, some equipment that required handling by multiple people in close proximity—such as spider dolly and track—could not be used. I happened to be teaching the final production course for seniors during one semester. In this course, students have the entire semester to shoot a documentary short.

The shorts the students created during that semester are distinctly identifiable as "pandemic films" due to the restrictions the students worked within. Those manifested themselves in content and/or production methods. That does not mean that the films are of lower quality. Working within the context of the pandemic required students to be (very) creative. Besides the industry and school restrictions, students had to consider their own feelings toward the pandemic and their living situations. Some lived with family members who were high risk. That also factored into their project topic and content. While it was frustrating for students to be limited by the pandemic—after all, most had been thinking about their final video project since sophomore year or so, and now that idea would have to be postponed—working within the pandemic context forced students to think about filmmaking differently. It forced them to be creative by approaching the stages of production differently. It also meant that faculty had to alter their mentorship approaches to help students find their voices under these changed conditions and problem solve differently to bring students' visions to life. In the end, students produced solid work that represents them under different restrictive circumstances than they had never experienced before. While I sincerely hope that they won't have to experience a similar situation in the future, should they be faced with novel challenges again, I hope that they will remember this experience. We can overcome challenges and/or restrictions creatively and successfully.

We can only imagine how Kiarostami would have responded to the pandemic creatively.

It is hoped that the following excerpt from *Lessons with Kiarostami*, edited by Paul Cronin and originally published in 2015, motivates you. The book is a compilation of transcripts from workshops Kiarostami gave over many years. Whether you are stuck with an idea for a film, are still awaiting inspiration, are in the middle of production, or are in the postproduction process, it is hoped that reading the following gives you the energy to complete whichever project you are currently working on and/or to take on the challenge Kiarostami lays out below. This is a task he gave his students in the workshops he conducted.

> Abbas Kiarostami:
> By day's end, I want you all to have at least one idea for a film you are going to make this week. At a previous workshop one participant made three films in two days. He had commendable ideas and brought with him a competent level of craft. Although he hadn't really thought things through, what I appreciated about him was that he never announced, "I'm going outside to make three films." He just appeared one morning

and screened them. He never complained about how he couldn't find a location or how one of his actors didn't show up or that he had absolutely no experience with the equipment he was using.

Over the years I have encountered participants at these meetings who are terrified about getting to work because they think that whatever they put their name to has to be a masterpiece. They should, as far as I can see, step back from this feeling and consider instead that making a series of self-contained sketches of average quality would be a useful exercise. Don't think you have to make films good enough to be screened at festivals. Focus your attention on producing a handful of small, truthful films of five minutes each rather than a single complex work. Everything is permitted, but short films—shot and edited the same day—are sufficient. I can't say that every film made during previous workshops was good, but it was important they were made. Perhaps each was a stepping stone to a stronger idea and a better film. If you don't have the tools to make big films, make small ones instead. We are all waiting for that open-minded producer to come along and finance our prized project. Until then, continue experimenting.

For a short, you only need one idea. My film *The Chorus* is seven minutes long and based on the simple concept that a man can't hear what is going on unless he is wearing a hearing aid. Don't complicate things. Don't waste a second. Cut to the chase. Sitting here, surrounded by colleagues, you shouldn't take five minutes to explain a five-minute film.... Search your mind to see what memories suggest themselves, then come back tomorrow with your ideas. What rises to the surface might not be too weighty, but we have to start somewhere. There is nothing wrong with walking out of this room right now with a camera but without a complete idea. An exercise is like a piece of paper. You can work on it and learn from it, then throw it away and move on. Answers are useful only in that they lead to new questions. Cinema is in a state of permanent evolution. It will forever be a quest, a journey. Every film is a stage on the road.

I have been thinking about what idea might connect your films and where there should be limitations imposed on your work here this week. In one previous workshop every participant made films involving a taxi, in another it was a cell phone, and in a third every film was inspired by Italian screenwriter Cesare Zavattini, who believed that all we need [to] do is look at the world around us for inspiration. For Zavattini, anyone can be the subject of a story. The people down there in the street are all we need for one hundred films. Workshop participants went outside and encountered complete strangers, the idea being that if you set up your camera in the middle of a crowd, the first person who walks past could be the perfect subject for a film. At a workshop in Tehran not long ago, we only had one single camera, angled on a passageway. Everyone took turns using it, stopping the first person who happened to walk by, which meant that everyone on screen came directly from real life. I could see participants exercising every ounce of their creativity to transform the circumstances that destiny had selected for them into intriguing and watchable films. In reminds me of prisoners, locked away, using plastic knives and dough to make sculptures, but who always succeed in creating something worthwhile.

As for self-imposed limitations this week, I have always thought an elevator would be a good location for a film. There is great potential for both drama and poetry when it comes to stories set in and around elevators. Within this enclosed room there is limited space, and presumably a film set in an elevator has to be of limited duration. Elevators make noise, some have interesting lighting, a few are ornate pieces of machinery, often there is music playing, and these days they have screens displaying information, news, and advertisements. There are many different kinds: public or private, for passengers or heavy goods, clean or dirty, mirrors on every wall, or none at all. Some have doors that open—to everyone's surprise—on both sides. Some are so small that three people can barely squeeze in, others are big enough to carry cars up and down buildings. Older elevators need someone to operate them, perhaps a distinguished, elderly gentleman who has spent his life travelling to and fro pushing buttons and pulling levers. Some trundle through decrepit buildings of only three or four floors, others fly at astonishing speed up and down moderns metal skyscrapers of one hundred storeys. Some are high-tech and completely silent, some make much noise. People are constantly getting on and off, which is a good way of introducing and ejecting characters. Personally, I feel naked and exposed whenever I am in an elevator, forced to stand beside people I don't know. How best to break the awkward silence? Elevators are inevitably what we encounter en route to and from places and people, which gives them a metaphoric quality. We could even make an action film in an elevator by introducing an assassin on the ground floor and a hero on the top. Most of you have probably already been inside an elevator today. They are environments we all immediately understand, so start considering the circumstances that might lead you to make use of these machines, and a great many stories and characters will doubtless reveal themselves.

Picture a young couple. He proposes to her and asks that she answer by the time they reach the top, so she presses all the buttons to give herself as much time as possible. The movement of the doors opening and closing can show the passage of time and elegantly build in a sense of suspense. How long will this trip take? Will she answer in time? Will it be the answer he is expecting? Another scenario: picture a two-year-old in a lift. The doors open and he has become a ten-year-old. As the elevator moves up the building, he gets older, until, by the top floor, he is a stoop-shouldered old man. And, of course, travelling in an elevator means being in close quarters with other people, something that requires a certain etiquette, which might serve as a narrative device. An elevator could clearly be the setting for a number of sketches and small dramas. The possibilities are endless. It's a magic box for stories, so start thinking about creating stories that are connected to elevators. If you don't like that particular restriction, think of a different location or a visual theme we can all shape our ideas around. But do it quickly. This is a workshop, so let's do some work. Don't squander your time here. The only wrongdoing is inactivity. Just get going and don't ask too many questions. The works will guide you. Saadi tells us it's better to walk in the desert aimlessly than to sit idly. Rumi writes that to work hard with no outcome is preferable to being asleep.

[A student points out to him that] "there are clear similarities between cars and elevators."

[Kiarostami responds:] "I had never thought of that. Yes, an elevator is a vertical car." (46–49)

As you read these lines, you are encouraged to get off the couch, to get out of your bed, to leave wherever you have been reading this book, put it aside and *take action*. Shoot and edit a short film in whatever time you have left available today. Seize the moment and experience the exercise Kiarostami laid out before us.

If you are hesitating, Kiarostami sympathizes: "There is no steeper learning curve than writing a scene, than filming that scene—again and again—so our work contains fewer and fewer errors. You bring an increasing level of skill to each version, and also to your next project. It's the evolution of technique" (46).

Get going, be inspired by Kiarostami, and enjoy the experience; the product outcome is secondary at this moment.

Additional Resources

Books (in English)

Abbott, Matthew. *Abbas Kiarostami and Film-Philosophy*. Edinburgh University Press, 2018.

Cardullo, Bert. *Out of Asia: The Films of Akira Kurosawa, Satyajit Ray, Abbas Kiarostami, and Zhang Yimou; Essays and Interviews*. Cambridge Scholars Publishing, 2008.

Cheshire, Godfrey. *Conversations with Kiarostami*, edited by Jim Colvill. The Film Desk, 2019.

Dabashi, Hamid. *Close Up: Iranian Cinema, Past, Present, and Future*. Verso, 2001.

Dönmez-Colin, Gönül. *Cinemas of the Other: A Personal Journey with Film-makers from the Middle East and Central Asia*. Intellect, 2012.

Elena, Alberto. *The Cinema of Abbas Kiarostami*. Saqi Books, 2005.

Harris, Mark E. *Inside Iran*. Chronicle Books, 2008.

Homayounpour, Gohar. *Doing Psychoanalysis in Tehran*. MIT Press, 2012.

Kiarostami, Abbas. *Abbas Kiarostami*. Hazan (Fernand) Editions, 2000.

Kiarostami, Abbas. *Abbas Kiarostami—Doors and Memories*. Nazar Publishing, 2015.

Kiarostami, Abbas. *Abbas Kiarostami—Snow Whites*. Nazar Publishing, 2011.

Kiarostami, Abbas. *Abbas Kiarostami—Trees & Crows*. Nazar Publishing, 2010.

Kiarostami, Abbas. *Abbas Kiarostami—The Wall*. Nazar Publishing, 2010.

Kiarostami, Abbas. *In the Shadow of Trees: The Collected Poetry of Abbas Kiarostami*. Translated by Iman Tavassoly and Paul Cronin, Sticking Place Books, 2016.

Kiarostami, Abbas. *Walking with the Wind (Voices and Visions in Film, 2)*. Bilingual edition, translated by Ahmad Karimi-Hakkak and Michael Beard, Harvard University Film Archive, 2002.

Kiarostami, Abbas. *Wind and Leaf*. Translated by Iman Tavassoly and Paul Cronin, Sticking Place Books, 2015.

Kiarostami, Abbas. *With the Wind*. Translated by Iman Tavassoly and Paul Cronin, Sticking Place Books, 2015.

Kiarostami, Abbas. *A Wolf on Watch*. Translated by Iman Tavassoly and Paul Cronin, Sticking Place Books, 2015.

Lessons with Kiarostami, edited by Paul Cronin, Sticking Place Books, 2015.

MacDonald, Scott. *The Sublimity of Document: Cinema as Diorama*. Oxford University Press, 2019.

Mulvey, Laura. *Death 24x a Second: Stillness and the Moving Image*. Reaktion Books, 2006.

My Sisters, Guard Your Veil; My Brother, Guard Your Eyes-Uncensored Iranian Voices, edited by Lila A. Zanganeh, Beacon Press, 2006.

Orgeron, Devin. *Road Movies—From Muybridge and Méliès to Lynch and Kiarostami*. Palgrave Macmillan, 2008.

Parks, Presley, P. Cronin, and M. Ciment. *Abbas Kiarostami Interviews*. Expressive Texts, 2020.

Perez, Gilberto. *The Material Ghost—Films and Their Medium*. John Hopkins University Press, 2000.

Rice, Julian. *Abbas Kiarostami's Cinema of Life: From "Homework" to "Like Someone in Love."* Rowman & Littlefield Publishers, 2020.

Reza Zani, Mahmoud. *Men at Work: Cinematic Lessons from Abbas Kiarostami*. Mhughes Press, 2013.

Journal Articles (mostly in English)

Abbott, Mathew. "The Appearance of Appearance: Absolute Truth in Abbas Kiarostami's *ABC Africa*." *Senses of Cinema*, no. 67, July 2013, p. 39.

Aufderheide, Pat. "Real Life Is More Important Than Cinema." *Cineaste*, vol. 21, no. 3, 1995, pp. 31–33.

Butler, Rex. "Abbas Kiarostami—The Shock of the Real." *Angelaki—Journal of the Theoretical Humanities*, vol. 17, no. 4, 2012, pp. 61–76.

Caputo, Rolando. "Five to *Ten*: Five Reflections on Abbas Kiarostami's *10*." *Senses of Cinema*, no. 29, December 2003, pp. 1–9.

Chamarette, Jenny. "Transitional Borders and Intermedial Spectacle: Kiarostami and Opera, between France and Iran." *Studies in French Cinema*, vol. 13, no. 3, 2013, pp. 257–71.

Cheshire, Godfrey. "Abbas Kiarostami—A Cinema of Questions." *Film Comment*, vol. 32, no. 4, July/August, 1996, pp. 34–43.

Cheshire, Godfrey. "How to Read Kiarostami." *Cineaste*, vol. 25, no. 4, 2000, pp. 8–15.

Cheshire, Godfrey. "In the City of Abbas." *Film Comment*, vol. 53, no. 6, November-December 2017, pp. 52–57.

Fairfax, Daniel. "The Wind Will Carry Him: Abbas Kiarostami Remembered (Introduction)." *Senses of Cinema*, no. 81, December 2016, pp. 1–2.

Grønstad, Asbjørn. "Abbas Kiarostami's *Shirin* and the Aesthetics of Ethical Intimacy." *Film Criticism*, vol. 37, no. 2, 2012, pp. 22–37.

Houssni, Joseph. "The Contingent-Generated Documentary." *Film International*, vol. 18, no. 1, March 2020, pp. 58–65.

Khodaei, Khatereh. "*Shirin* as Described by Kiarostami." *Offscreen*, vol. 13, no. 1, 2009, offscreen.com/view /Shirin_kiarostami. Accessed 26 Nov. 2021.

Knox, Jim. "Cacti Blossom in a Desert: Some Short Films of Abbas Kiarostami." *Senses of Cinema*, no. 29, December 2003, www.sensesofcinema.com/2003/abbas-kiarostami/kiarostami_shorts/. Accessed 26 Nov. 2021.

Köhler, U., and B. Heisenberg. "Interview: Abbas Kiarostami." *Revolver*, vol. 10, 2003, www.revolver-film .com/hefte/heft-10-kiarostami/. Accessed 26 Nov. 2021.

Krzych, Scott. "Auto-Motivations: Digital Cinema and Kiarostami's Relational Aesthetics." *The Velvet Light Trap*, no. 66, Fall 2010, pp. 26–35.

Lippard, Chris. "Disappearing into the Distance and Getting Closer All the Time: Vision, Position and Thought in Kiarostami's *The Wind Will Carry Us*." *Journal of Film and Video*, vol. 61, no. 4, Winter 2009, pp. 31–40.

Lopate, Phillip. "Kiarostami Close Up." *Film Comment*, vol. 32, no. 4, Jul-Aug. 1996, pp. 37–40.

Mahani, Najmeh K. "An Interview with Abbas Kiarostami and Aydin Aghdashloo—Talking about Poetry, Life, Death, Art and Politics." *Offscreen*, vol. 21, no. 7, July 2017, offscreen.com/view/an-interview-with-abbas-kiarostami-and-aydin-aghdashloo. Accessed 26 Nov. 2021.

Maimon, Vered. "Beyond Representation—Abbas Kiarostami's and Predo Costa's Minor Cinema." *Third Text*, vol. 26, no. 3, May 2012, pp. 331–44.

Mehrnaz Saeed-Vafa. "Drinking from a Mirage." *Senses of Cinema*, no. 81, December 2016, pp. 1–8.

Mehrnaz Saeed-Vafa. "Kiarostami, Abbas." *Senses of Cinema*, no. 81, December 2016, pp. 1–29.

Mitha, Farouk. "Review Essay—The Films of Abbas Kiarostami: Framing the Burdens of Contemporary Muslim Identities." *Arab Studies Quarterly*, vol. 31, no. 1&2, Winter/Spring, 2009, pp. 141–48.

Montinari, Mazzino. "Abbas Kiarostami—Director." *Cineuropa.org*, 22 Nov. 2001. cineuropa.org/en/interview/17446/. Accessed 26 Nov. 2021.

Mulvey, Laura. "Kiarostami's Uncertainty Principle." *Sight and Sound*, vol. 8, no. 6, June 1998, pp. 24–27.

Mulvey, Laura. "Repetition and Return—The Spectator's Memory in Abbas Kiarostami's Koker Trilogy." *Third Text*, vol. 21, no. 1, 2007, pp. 19–29.

Nancy, Jean-Luc. "On Evidence: 'Life and Nothing More,' by Abbas Kiarostami." *Discourse*, vol. 21, no 1, 1999, pp. 76–87.

Rist, Peter. "Meeting Abbas Kiarostami—The 24th Montreal World Film Festival." *Offscreen*, vol. 5, no. 2, 2001, offscreen.com/view/Kiarostami. Accessed 26 Nov. 2021.

Saeedi, Pouneh. "Female Figurations in Kiarostami's *The Wind Will Carry Us*." *Canadian Journal of Film Studies*, vol. 22, no. 2, Fall 2013, pp. 81–96.

Saljoughi, Sara. "Seeing, Iranian Style: Women and Collective Vision in Abbas Kiarostami's *Shirin*." *Iranian Studies*, vol. 45, no. 4, 2012, pp. 519–35.

Slaymaker, James. "Cinema Never Dies: Abbas Kiarostami's '24 Frames' and the Ontology of the Digital Image." *Senses of Cinema*, no. 92, October 2019, www.sensesofcinema.com/2019/feature-articles/cinema-never-dies-abbas-kiarostamis-24-frames-and-the-ontology-of-the-digital-image/. Accessed 26 Nov. 2021.

Sterritt, David. "The Element of Chance." *Film Comment*, vol. 52, no. 5, September-October, 2016, pp. 94–95.

Sterritt, David. "With Borrowed Eyes: An Interview with Abbas Kiarostami." *Film Comment*, vol. 36, no. 4, July-August 2000, pp. 20–26.

Stiegler, Bernard. "On Abbas Kiarostami 'Close Up.'" *Parrhesia*, no. 20, 2014, pp. 40–48.

Tabarraee, Babak. "Abbas Kiarostami: A Cinema of Silence." *The Soundtrack*, vol. 5, no. 1, 2012, pp. 5–13.

Utterson, Andrew. "On the Movie Theater as Haunted Space: Spectral Spectatorship and Existential Historiography in Abbas Kiarostami's *Shirin* (2008)." *Quarterly Review of Film and Video*, vol. 33, no. 8, 2016, pp. 685–706.

Zahedi, Farshad. "Who Are You, Mr. Kiarostami? Koker Trilogy and European Critics and Scholars." *Quarterly Review of Film and Video*, Vol. 35, no. 8, 2018, pp. 741–61.

Video Resources

"Abbas Kiarostami—An IU Cinema Exclusive." *YouTube*, uploaded by IUCinema, 21 Jul. 2014, www.youtube.com/watch?v=neYgsuUC8pw.

"Abbas Kiarostami in Conversation with. . . ." *YouTube*, uploaded by TIFF Originals, 5 Jul. 2016, www.youtube.com/watch?v=-1CCPg5UY-E.

Abbas Kiarostami: The Art of Living. Directed by Pat Collins and Fergus Daly, 2003. *Vimeo*, uploaded by Experimental Film Society, 5 Jul. 2016, vimeo.com/173519394.

Kiarostami, Abbas. "10 on Ten." *YouTube*. Uploaded by Firouzan Films, 2008+2009. "Pt. 1." www.youtube.com/watch?v=RPiVi3BTdqs.

Kiarostami, Abbas. "10 on Ten." *YouTube*. Uploaded by Firouzan Films, 2008+2009. "Pt. 3." www.youtube.com/watch?v=QjSc6_fsIIY.

Kiarostami, Abbas. "10 on Ten." *YouTube*. Uploaded by Firouzan Films, 2008+2009. "Pt. 9–1." www.youtube.com/watch?v=Y9xO2kwzpZQ.

Kiarostami, Abbas. "10 on Ten." *YouTube*. Uploaded by Firouzan Films, 2008+2009. "Pt. 9–2." www.youtube.com/watch?v=ihccWT_8NgM.

"Kiarostami on Making of Five." *YouTube*, uploaded by Haridas B., 17 Jun. 2008, www.youtube.com/watch?v=xu9cbCJKLs8.

Making of "Like Someone in Love." Directed by Morteza Farshbaf. The Criterion Collection, 2012.

"NYFF Press Conference: Like Someone in Love." *YouTube*, uploaded by Film at Lincoln Center, 20 Dec. 2012, www.youtube.com/watch?v=UFXyyBIDIAU.

"Open Conversation with Abbas Kiarostami." *YouTube*, uploaded by Maxwell School of Syracuse University, 3 Apr. 2014, www.youtube.com/watch?v=4d4qrkm061E.

Roads of Kiarostami. Directed by Abbas Kiarostami. 2005.

Taste of Shirin. Directed by Hamideh Razavi, 2008. *YouTube*, uploaded by Sayantan Dutta, 20 Jun. 2020, www.youtube.com/watch?v=IkeBDYryepk.

10 on Ten. Directed by Abbas Kiarostami. 2004.

"Tribute to Abbas Kiarostami." *YouTube*, uploaded by Peter Scarlet, 21+22 Jul. 2016, Part 1, www.youtube.com/watch?v=yRLUqcHIBxc.

"Tribute to Abbas Kiarostami." *YouTube*, uploaded by Peter Scarlet, 21+22 Jul. 2016, Part 2, www.youtube.com/watch?v=3WGF4lgyhVM.

"Tribute to Abbas Kiarostami." *YouTube*, uploaded by Peter Scarlet, 21+22 Jul. 2016, Part 3, www.youtube.com/watch?v=_D4O7G6gZqw.

"Tribute to Abbas Kiarostami." *YouTube*, uploaded by Peter Scarlet, 21+22 Jul. 2016, Part 4, www.youtube.com/watch?v=3o-BSPJzVSs.

"The Modern School of Film with Abbas Kiarostami." *YouTube*, uploaded by The Modern School of Film, 5 Jul. 2016, www.youtube.com/watch?v=cKCabzXgxso.

A Walk with Kiarostami. Directed by Jamsheed Akrami, 2001. *YouTube*, uploaded by lachambreverte, 18 Feb. 2018, www.youtube.com/watch?v=KKoSoL_jIWE.

A Week with Kiarostami. Directed by Yuji Mohara, 1999. *YouTube*, uploaded by Sayantan Dutta, 11 Jun. 2020, www.youtube.com/watch?v=0-U3xFmPqUs (Part 1).

A Week with Kiarostami. Directed by Yuji Mohara, 1999. *YouTube*, uploaded by Sayantan Dutta, 11 Jun. 2020, www.youtube.com/watch?v=u9CTskB_Bhc (Part 2).

Also, *The Criterion Channel*, www.criterionchannel.com/videos/, hosts many materials on Abbas Kiarostami.

Index

Abbas Kiarostami: The Art of Living, viii, ix, xiv, xxvii, xxxii
Abbas Kiarostami: Truth and Dreams, xxiii, xxxvi
ABC Africa, xxii, xxxii, 66, 83; filmmaking abroad, xviii; film technique, xxv–xxvi, 46–47
And Life Goes On, xvi–xvii, xxxv, 46, 65, 83; opening scene in, 38–39. *See also* Koker trilogy
A Propos de Nice, La Suite, xviii

Big Heat, The, 27
Binoche, Juliette: *Certified Copy*, 67, 69, 75–76, 79, 80, 84; *Shirin*, xxix, 66
Bread and Alley, xv, 35

Cannes International Film Festival, xxii, 3–4, 28, 74; Catherine Deneuve, xix, 84; Jafar Panahi, 77; *Taste of Cherry*, xvii, xix, 20, 25, 28, 79, 84, 85; *Ten*, xxiii, xxvii, 42; *24 Frames*, xxxi
Case #1, Case #2, xix
censorship, xix–xx
Certified Copy, 66–71, 75, 78, 79–81; filmmaking abroad, xx, xxii; neorealism in, ix
Children of Heaven, 25
Citizen Kane, 40
Classe Tous Risques, 28

Close-Up, xvii, 3, 8, 49, 58, 63, 65, 83; film technique, xxiii, 4, 45–46; interpretation of, 7; Koker trilogy, 11–14; title, 5

Deneuve, Catherine, xix, 84, 86
Dental Hygiene, 4

Farrokhzad, Forugh, 34–35
Five Dedicated to Ozu, xxii, 50–59, 66, 71; censorship in, 73; film technique, 48, 49n5

Ganjavi, Nezami, 61
Goodbye South, Goodbye, 30

Homework, xxxviin8, 3, 4, 8, 31, 66
Hou, Hsiao-hsien, 30
How the Myth Was Made: A Study of Robert Flaherty's "Man of Aran," xxxiii

Institute for the Intellectual Development of Children and Young Adults, xv, xxxviin8, 4, 10, 19, 35; as Kanun Parvaresh Fekri, xvii
Iranian Revolution, xix, xxi, 3, 54; attending the cinema, 8, 9n1; filmmaking, 6, 52, 58; photography, 35

Kanun Parvaresh Fekri. *See* Institute for the Intellectual Development of Children and Young Adults
Karmitz, Martin, 49

Kiarostami, Abbas: on "An Unfinished Cinema," x–xi, xxxii, 27, 32, 51, 80; on art, xiv, xx, 5, 77, 79–80; on audience, x–xiii, xxii, xxxiii, 14, 31, 61–62; on awards, 28; on casting non-professional actors, 56; on children and childhood, xvi–xvii; on *Close-Up*, xxiii, 5–6, 63; on commercial films, 28, 51; on copy vs. original, 68; on creativity, 76–77; on digital equipment in filmmaking, 46–48, 59; on directing, 12–13; on dreaming, xi, 16–17; on editing, 6; on exploring dreams in cinema, 28; on female characters, 13, 25, 63; on filming *Five*, 52–53, 71; on filming women in Iran, 8; on filmmaking, xviii, xxiv, xxv–xxvi, xxx, xxxii, 89–92; on filmmaking in Iran, 25, 73, 78, 84; on film unions, 31; on funding films, 42–43, 49; on humanity, 36–37; on Iranian audience, 17–18, 51; on Iranian cinema, 25–26, 72; on Iranian government, xix–xx, xxi, 25, 58–59, 72, 77; on love, xxxvi, 69; on lying and truth in filmmaking, 11, 14–15, 17; on making *Taste of Cherry*, 39, 53–54; on male characters, 13; on music, xi; on nature, 27, 36, 52; on non-professional actors in *Close-Up*, 45–46; on photography, xxxiii–xxxiv, 35–36, 48; on photography and audience, 35–36; on political films, 40; on realism and viewers, 56; on restrictions, xx–xxi, 7–8, 17, 43, 55, 58; on roads, xiv–xv; on running, 40–41; on script writing, 12, 32, 58; on setting a goal, xxxvi; on start in film industry, 19, 24, 74; on storytelling, 35, 48–49, 80; on *Taste of Cherry*, xi–xiii, 24, 26, 32–33, 54, 55–56; on *Ten*, xxiii–xxiv, xxvi–xxvii, 55; on themes in his work, 36; on *The Wind Will Carry Us*, 39–40; on violence in cinema, 27–28; on watching films, 48, 63; on working with children, 17, 18–19; on working with non-professional actors, 12, 19, 32–33, 45; on writing *Through the Olive Trees*, 44–45
Kiarostami, Ahmad, xxxi
Koker trilogy, 10, 11–15, 16, 26, 54; as three films, 26
Kurosawa, Akira, 35

Lang, Fritz, 27
Life Goes On. See *And Life Goes On*; Koker trilogy
Like Someone in Love, xx, xxii
Lloyd Webber, Andrew, xxxviiin19
Loach, Ken, 46

Majidi, Majid, 25
Making of "Like Someone in Love," xxxviiin19
Man of Aran, xxxiii
Mirror, 25
mk2, xviii

Naderi, Amir, 41, 84–85
neorealism, ix, 56, 66, 82

Panahi, Jafar/Dschafar, 25, 72–74, 77–78
Persian Carpet, xxxiv

Olmi, Ermanno, 46

Red Hat and the Cousin, The, 18
Report, The, ix, xv, 67, 69–70
Roads of Kiarostami, xiv–xv, 52
Rumi (Persian poet), 32, 62, 68, 92
Runner, The, 41, 84

Sautet, Claude, 28
Shahabazi, Parwiz, 25
Shirin, xxii, xxxii, 61–64, 66; film technique, xxvii, xxviii, xxx, xxxviiin15

So Can I, xv
Some Ideas on the Cinema, viii–ix
Sound of Music, The, xxx
Star Wars, 43

Talk to Her, xxxviiin10
Taste of Cherry (*A Taste of Cherry* and *The Taste of Cherry*), viii, xix, xxii, 29, 39, 65, 79; Cannes, xvii, 25, 84, 85; censorship of, xx–xxi, 73; cultural representation in, 31–32, 40, 55–56; ending of, xi–xiii, xxxv, 20–23, 24, 47, 53–54; film technique, xxiv–xxv, 32; Koker trilogy, 26; suicide in, 26–27, 33
Taste of Shirin, xxvii–xxx, xxxviiin15
Ten, xxii, 42–43, 46, 55, 59; censorship of, 73; film technique, xxiii–xxiv, xxvi–xxvii, 47. See also *10 on Ten*
10 on Ten, xxxviiin13, 56, 66, 73
Through the Olive Trees, 11–15, 44, 46, 54, 65, 79; audience, 31, 62; opening sequence, xxxviiin12; questioning ideology in, xiv. See also Koker trilogy

Tickets, xviii, 73
Traveler, The, xvi, 40, 65
Traveller from the South, 25
24 Frames, xxii, xxxi, xxxviiin19
Two Solutions for One Problem, xv

"Unfinished Cinema, An," x–xi

Walk with Kiarostami, A, xxii, xxxiii–xxxv, xxxvi
Where Is the Friend's Home?, 3, 4, 16, 26. See also *Where's the Friend's House?*
Where's the Friend's House? (*Where Is the Friend's House?*), xvi, xvii, 3, 4, 10, 58, 65, 79; Amir Naderi, 84–85; analysis of, 39; Kiarostami's perspective on cast of, 11, 16; narrative, 57. See also Koker trilogy
Wind Will Carry Us, The, xxxii, 34, 35, 46, 65; analysis of, 39; censorship of, 73; ending of, 60; Kurdistan, 40

Zavattini, Cesare, viii, 90

About the Editor

Monika Raesch is associate professor of film studies and video production at Suffolk University. She edited *Margarethe von Trotta: Interviews* in the Conversations with Filmmakers Series published by University Press of Mississippi, and she has published articles in such journals as the *Journal of Film and Video* and *Feminist Media Studies*. She also edits video work for clients.

www.ingramcontent.com/pod-product-compliance
Lightning Source LLC
Chambersburg PA
CBHW022105160426
43198CB00008B/353